Python Programming

for Engineers and Scientists

Irfan Turk

Edited by
Ibrahim Emre Celikkale

Python Programming for Engineers and Scientists

Printed in the United States of America.
ISBN-13: 978-1543173833
ISBN-10: 1543173837

PREFACE

Python is a high level programming language which has an increasing reputation during the last few decades. It was originally created by Guido van Rossum, and first released in February 1991. The language was developed under an open source license administered by the Python Software Foundation (PSF). It can be freely distributed and used by programmers under many operating systems.

The programming language has an easy to use syntax that makes the language very straightforward to learn and grasp. Unlike some other famous programming languages such as C, C++, or Java, there is no need to pre-define the data types of the variables. The variables are created as they are used in Python, which often requires less coding to carry out the tasks.

Python addresses the problems of many people from a wide range of areas including all fields of engineering branches, mathematicians, physicists, computer scientists, and even programmers from social sciences. It has applications regarding web and internet development, databases, software development, scientific and numerical computing, digital image processing, graphical user interfaces and some others that attract many users from different backgrounds and areas of study.

Although this book is aimed at teaching Python as a computer programming course for one semester in colleges and universities, it is also a nice resource and textbook for individual learners providing a complete collection of written and tested codes along with applications. If there arise any questions or recommendations, please feel free to send an e-mail to iturkbooks@gmail.com.

Teaching Python as a programming language is explained in the first part of the book. In the second part, object-oriented programming and working with databases are dealt with as part of an attempt for software engineering concentration. In the third and the last part, some of the selected topics that are essential for engineers and scientists are covered. The topics considered in the last part include Matrix Algebra, Plotting Graphics, Symbolic Calculations, Introduction to Statistics, Numerical Methods, Digital Image Processing, and Graphical User Interfaces.

The author of this book has been teaching mathematics and computer programming courses in secondary schools and universities for more than 10 years. In this regard, the book is prepared considering the pedagogical approach for teaching a subject. The book provides 117 illustrative and instructive examples including the solutions along with the codes. The reader can easily modify and update the presented codes depending on their needs.

ABOUT THE AUTHOR

Dr. Irfan Turk is a mathematician who has worked as a math and computer programming teacher in middle schools, high schools, and universities for more than 10 years. Dr. Turk earned his B.S. degree from Fatih University, M.S. degree from The University of Texas at Arlington, and PhD. from Istanbul University all in mathematics. His research interests include but are not limited to numerical solutions of differential equations, scientific computing, mathematical modeling, and programming in Python and MATLAB.

ACKNOWLEDGMENTS

I would like to mention and thank a few people who helped me in the preparation of this book.

First of all, I would like to express my special appreciation and grateful thanks to my colleague and friend Ibrahim Emre Celikkale, who accepted to be the editor of this book. His recommendations regarding the language of the book, and its presentation were of supreme importance to me.

Next, I would like to mention a few names and give credits about their nice works from which I learned a lot about Python. I would like to thank Dr. Charles Severance from the University of Michigan for his instructive courses about Python on youtube.com and coursera.org. I would also like to thank Derek Banas, Bucky Roberts, and Mustafa Murat Coskun for their helpful and instructive videos about Python on youtube.com.

And finally, I would like to thank my dear wife, Maksude, for her unwavering support and understanding, and for always being there.

Irfan Turk, PhD

Contents

Part I

FUNDAMENTALS OF PYTHON

Chapter 1

INTRODUCTION TO PYTHON

Python 3 programming language will be explained in this work. Python version 3.5.2 is used to test the codes and scripts.

Python holds an open source license (administered by Python Software Foundation) which makes the language free to use and accessible to anyone. The software has a simple syntax that yields shorter programs compared to other popular languages such as C, C++, or Java. Python can be used in a wide range of applications due to its large standard library and remarkable number of modules. Therefore, it attracts many users and is one of the best choices for engineers and scientists in various scientific and computational applications.

In this chapter, installation of the Python software will be explained as an introduction. Next, we will take a look at the modules of the language. Then, the following topics will be handled: Using Python as a calculator, variables and expressions, overview of data types, operators, built-in functions, and formatting outputs.

1.1 Installing Python

In this section, we will show how to install Python on a PC. One can find the most recent version of the software at https://www.python.org/downloads/. As will be seen on the web page, it is available for various operating systems. After the version that fits your operating system is selected and downloaded, it can be installed on your computer.

While installation, it is highly recommended to click on "Add Python 3.x to PATH" check button. Here, 3.x is the version that you try to install. If this option is checked, one can run programs from the command window after the installation of Python (or Python interpreter). Once the command window is opened, type python, and then Python shell will be ready to start programming. You can type your commands next to "⋙" symbol, which is called the "prompt".

```
C:\Users\Lenovo>python
Python 3.5.2 (v3.5.2:4def2a2901a5, Jun 25 2016, 22:01:18) [MSC v.1900 32
bit (Intel)] on win32
Type "help", "copyright", "credits" or "license" for more information.
>>>
```

Figure 1.1: Running Python from Command window in Windows operating system.

After installing Python, one can also click on IDLE, which stands for **I**nteractive **D**eve**L**opment **E**nvironment, to run the codes.

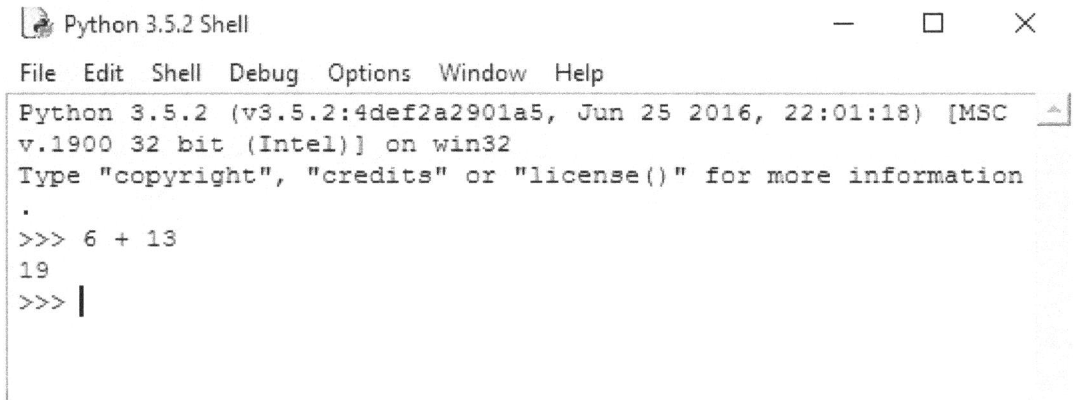

Figure 1.2: IDLE running on a Windows operating system

The IDLE environment having extra buttons on it is also called an interactive shell.

In the Python IDLE , if you click on File ⇒ New File button, the following editor will be popped up.

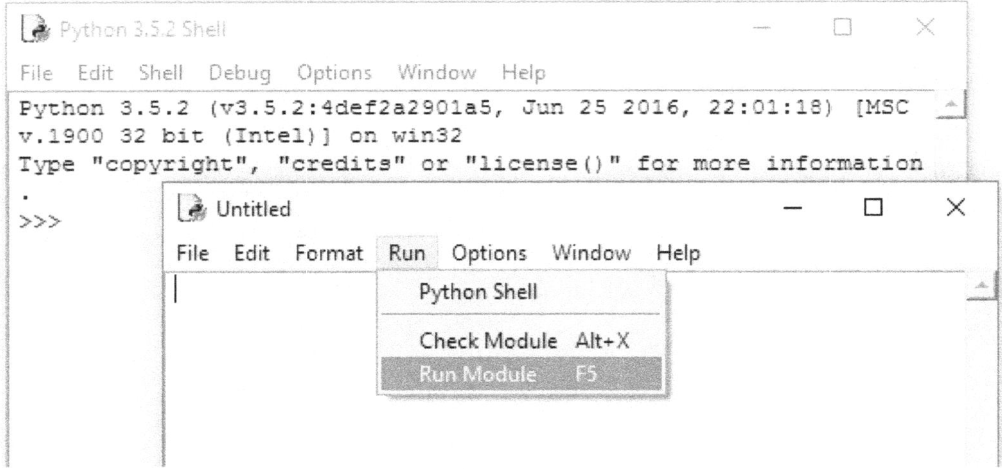

Figure 1.3: Python IDLE editor

Coding can be achieved using the editor, and then, one can save them by adding the extension .py (Name.py) making it a Python file. Then, click on Run ⇒ Run Module buttons to run the codes within the editor.

There are several nice editors available to edit and run new codes. If the keywords "Python Editor" is searched on Google, one can find plenty of them. Some of these editors have nice features such as coloring the scripts, assisting the user with completing the codes, etc. The reader is recommended to use PyCharm and Pydev as a Python editor.

1.2 Using Modules in Python

A module is a file composed of Python definitions and expressions. Modules are very useful packages that set the syntax of built-in functions available with that module.

Throughout this book, various modules will be used depending on the subject. Before using a module, it should be imported to the program.

After importing a module, i.e. math, one can find out some information regarding the module by using the **help()** function as below.

```
>>> import math
>>> help(math)
Help on built-in module math:

NAME
    math

DESCRIPTION
    This module is always available.  It provides access to the
    mathematical functions defined by the C standard.

FUNCTIONS
    acos(...)
        acos(x)

        Return the arc cosine (measured in radians) of x.
...
...
```

To check the names that are defined by a module, **dir()** function may be used after importing the module as shown below.

```
>>> import math
>>> dir(math)
['__doc__', '__loader__', '__name__', '__package__', '__spec__', 'acos',
'acosh', 'asin', 'asinh', 'atan', 'atan2', 'atanh', 'ceil', 'copysign',
'cos', 'cosh', 'degrees', 'e', 'erf', 'erfc', 'exp', 'expm1', 'fabs',
'factorial', 'floor', 'fmod', 'frexp', 'fsum', 'gamma', 'gcd', 'hypot',
'inf', 'isclose', 'isfinite', 'isinf', 'isnan', 'ldexp', 'lgamma', 'log',
'log10', 'log1p', 'log2', 'modf', 'nan', 'pi', 'pow', 'radians', 'sin',
```

```
'sinh', 'sqrt', 'tan', 'tanh', 'trunc']
>>>
```

In order to use the functions that are defined within the module, it is necessary to write the module name followed by a dot, and the name of the function.

As an example, if the user wants to calculate the value of $\sin(\frac{\pi}{2})$, he/she may type

```
>>> import math
>>> math.sin(math.pi/2)
1.0
>>>
```

There is another way of adding $\sin(x)$ function and a constant π as follows:

```
>>> from math import sin
>>> from math import pi
>>> sin(pi/2)
1.0
>>>
```

In this case, it is required to use the words "from" and "import" to calculate the same value.

1.3 Using Python as a Calculator

Python can be used as a big calculator, as well. In Python interactive shell, if the user types $\ggg$ 2 + 3 at the prompt and hit enter, the result is shown on the screen. Similar operations can be carried on in a similar manner. Several examples of these operations are listed below:

```
>>> 2 + 3
5
>>> 5 - 8
-3
```

```
>>> 7 * 4
28
>>> 4 / 5
0.8
>>> 2**3
8
>>> 24//5
4
>>>
```

In the above example, double star "**" represents the power operator. It corresponds to **pow()**, a built-in math function in Python.

Another operator is about rounding the number to the nearest smallest integer which can be applied by using double slashes. It corresponds to **floor()**, a built-in math function. If 24 is divided by 5, the result is 4.8. If 4.8 is rounded to the smallest integer, the result is obtained as 4.

To use such other operations as taking the square root of a number, or using exponential functions, one needs to import the math module.

Example 1.1 Find the result of $5 + \frac{7}{9} + 4\cos(\pi)$ with Python.

Solution. The following code may be used to find the result.

```
>>> import math
>>> 5 + (7 / 9) * math.cos(math.pi)
4.222222222222222
>>>
```

◀

Once a module is imported, it is not needed to import it again for additional usages or calculations during the same session.

Example 1.2 Find the result of $y = \frac{100}{e^4} + 4\sqrt{23}$.

Solution. The following code can be typed at prompt to find the result.

```
>>> (100 / (math.exp(4))) + math.sqrt(23)
6.627395412186138
>>>
```

◀

1.4 Variables and Expressions

After calculating a result, one may need to use the value of that result for subsequent calculations as well. In that case, it is a better idea to store these values under some structures called variables. We give names to functions, modules, or variables that certain values are assigned. In the literature, these names are called *identifiers*. Any value contained in variables or functions is called an expression. Something does not necessarily need to be evaluated in all expressions.

There are certain names, or identifiers that are reserved to the Python language. These keywords cannot be used as regular names. Since Python is a case sensitive language, these names (or identifiers) must be spelled correctly if they are to be used for other purposes. One can find out these keywords by using the **kwlist** function in **keyword** module as shown in the following code:

```
>>> import keyword
>>> keyword.kwlist
['False', 'None', 'True', 'and', 'as', 'assert', 'break', 'class',
'continue', 'def', 'del', 'elif', 'else', 'except', 'finally', 'for',
'from', 'global', 'if', 'import', 'in', 'is', 'lambda', 'nonlocal',
'not', 'or', 'pass', 'raise', 'return', 'try', 'while', 'with', 'yield']
>>>
```

Example 1.3 Check whether any of the following names is a keyword or not. “Howareyou”, “and”

Solution. By using **iskeyword** function from keyword **module**, we can check the first name ”Howareyou” as following.

```
>>> import keyword
>>> keyword.iskeyword("Howareyou")
False
>>>
```

Note that the result is False, meaning that the entered name is not a keyword. Similarly, the word "and" can be checked as follows:

```
>>> from keyword import iskeyword as isk
>>> isk("and")
True
>>>
```

◀

In the previous program, the structure of the code should be kept as it is. The only term that can be altered is the "isk" term. Notice that the result is turned out to be "True", meaning that the word that we just checked is a keyword.
In some programming languages such as C, C++, or Java, the types of the variables should be defined. In Python, this is not the case. Variables can be immediately used as they are assigned corresponding values. This property often makes the code shorter compared to other languages.

There are certain rules that need to be considered when giving names to variables or identifiers.

The name should start with either a letter or an underscore ("_" character). The remainder of the name may be composed of letters, numbers, or underscores.

Example 1.4 Check whether it is permissible to use the following names as a variable name. "Hola", "15Good", "Alex+Huns", "Nice_Job", "WhatisWrong?", "Che_ese2017"

Solution. It can be checked whether a name is valid to be a variable or identifier name or not by using the **isidentifier()** function as follows:

```
>>> 'Hola'.isidentifier()
True
>>> "15Good".isidentifier()
```

```
False
>>> "Alex+Hunt".isidentifier()
False
>>> "Nice_Job".isidentifier()
True
>>> "WhatisWrong?".isidentifier()
False
>>> "Che_ese2017".isidentifier()
True
>>>
```

◀

As it can be seen above, the names that turn out **True** are permissible to be a variable name. We can place the words between quotation marks, or apostrophes. Both are acceptable in Python.

If we consider the structure of 'Hola'.isidentifier(), we see that there is a string, then a dot, and finally a function. We may think of dot "." as an operator. What it performs is that, it applies the function following the dot to the string preceding it. This structure will be frequently used throughout the book.

Example 1.5 In a given equation, $P * V = n * R * T$, some of the variables are as follows: $P = 10$, $n = 2$, $R = 7$, and $T = 4$. Write a code that calculates the unknown parameter V.

Solution. First, we may assign the given values to the variables. Then, the unknown V can be determined from $V = (n * R * T)/P$ as shown in the following program:

```
>>> P, n, R, T = 10, 2, 7, 4
>>> V = (n * R * T ) / P
>>> V
5.6
>>>
```

◀

Note that, the variables can be defined in one row by separating them with a comma to make the code more compact, as shown in the program above. The known variables can also be as-signed in a separate row for each one, as well. But, that makes the code longer. After calculating V, if you type V and hit enter, you can see the value of the variable V.

1.5 Overview of Core Data Types

There are different types of data in Python. These data types will be briefly introduced in this section in order to make the reader familiar with them. In Chapter 5, we will elaborate on the examination of these data types. There are six standard data types in Python. These include Numbers, Strings, Booleans, Lists, Tuples and Dictionaries.

1.5.1 Numbers

There are two types of numbers; namely *integers* and *floats*.

```
>>> x = 4
>>> type(x)
<class 'int'>
>>> y = 3.5
>>> type(y)
<class 'float'>
>>>
```

In order to find out the data type of a number, we use the **type()** function. As seen above, 4 is assigned to the variable x, and 3.5 is assigned to y. Python automatically concludes that x is an integer, and y is a float number. Once you check the classes of these numbers, you can see that they are marked as 'int' which stands for integer, and 'float' obviously meaning a float number.

1.5.2 Strings

A string is a series of characters saved to the memory in the form of text. In python, one can assign strings to variables by using quotation marks, or apostrophes, or by putting the text inside the **str()** function as shown in the following.

```
>>> Str1 = "This is a string"
>>> Str2 = 'This is also a string'
>>> Str3 = str("2017 is another string")
>>> type(Str1)
<class 'str'>
>>> type(Str2)
<class 'str'>
>>> type(Str3)
<class 'str'>
>>>
```

The number of characters from which a data is composed of may be checked by using the **len()** function.

```
>>> len(Str1)
16
>>> len(Str3)
22
>>>
```

As can be seen above, Str1 possesses 16 characters. We can get inside of these strings by using square brackets.

```
>>> Str1[2]
'i'
>>> Str1[0:5]
'This '
>>> Str1[6:]
's a string'
>>> Str1[-5:]
'tring'
>>>
```

Indexing starts with zero (0) in Python. Therefore, Str1[2] means the 3rd element of the string Str1. Similarly, Str1[0:5] yields all elements of Str1 from the 1st element to the 5th; Str1[6:] yields all elements of Str1 from the 7th to the last element. We can reach the elements in the reverse order, as well. For example, Str1[-5:] yields all elements of Str1 from the last 5th element up to the last element.

Strings may be concatenated by adding them up as follows:

```
>>> Str1 = "Hello"
>>> Str2 = "World"
>>> Str1+Str2
'HelloWorld'
>>>
```

As it is seen, by using the plus (+) sign, strings are concatenated without any space between them.

The function **print()** is another important built-in function to print data on the screen.

```
>>> print(Str1)
This is a string
>>>
```

By using the print() function, we can also concatenate strings as shown in the following.

```
>>> Str1="Alexander"
>>> Str2="Friend"
>>> print(Str2,Str1)
Friend Alexander
>>>
```

As shown above, by using the **print()** function, a space is inserted between the strings.

Example 1.6 Three strings are given as St1 = "My Big Brother", St2 = "Sports Club", St3 = "Barcelona Nice". By using these three strings given, obtain the new string "Big Club Barcelona".

Solution. We may write the following piece of code at prompt to get the required string.

```
>>> St1 = "My Big Brother"
>>> St2 = "Sports Club"
>>> St3 = "Barcelona Nice"
>>> Get_Str = str(St1[3:6]+" "+St2[7:]+" "+St3[0:9])
>>> print(Get_Str)
Big Club Barcelona
>>>
```

◄

1.5.3 Booleans

Boolean values are used to represent truth values as True, or False. Function **bool()** can be used to return a Boolean value.

```
>>> bool(3<5)
True
>>> bool(10>20)
False
>>>
```

We may want return Boolean values while checking a string for different purposes, as well.

```
>>> St1 = "This is NICE"
>>> St2 = "2017"
>>> St3 = "WOW"
>>> St4 = "Year 12345"
>>> St1.isalnum() #check if all characters of St1 are numbers
False
>>> St2.isdigit() # check if St2 has all digits
True
>>> St3.isupper() #check if characters of St3 are all upper case
True
```

```
>>> St4.endswith('5') # check if St4 ends with string 5
True
>>>
```

As it is seen above, the character "#" is used to leave a comment in Python. Whatever you write after the "#" symbol is ignored.

1.5.4 Lists

Lists are very important data types in Python. We can create arrays or matrices using lists. These topics will be covered in Chapter 5.

Lists are enclosed with square brackets [ ].

```
>>> MyList=[1,2,3,'Banana','Orange']
>>> type(MyList)
<class 'list'>
>>> MyList=([1,2,3,'Banana','Orange'])
>>> type(MyList)
<class 'list'>
>>>
```

As we can see above, we can use square brackets inside parentheses or square brackets alone to define a list.

To get data from a list, indexing may be used.

```
>>> MyList[2]
3
>>> MyList[3][1:5]
'anan'
>>>
```

We can delete any of the items of the list by using **del** function. We can delete the 4th element of MyList as follows.

```
>>> del MyList[3]
>>> MyList
```

```
[1, 2, 3, 'Orange']
>>>
```

After the **del** command,we need to put a space, and then the item we want to remove from the list.

There are some useful functions available to work with the lists.

Table 1.1: Some of the available functions used with the lists

Function	**Explanation**
ListName.append(x)	adds the item x to the end of the list called ListName
ListName.count(x)	returns how many times the item x appears from the list called ListName
ListName.index(x)	returns the index of the first appeared item x from the list called ListName
ListName.insert(i, x)	inserts the item x after the ith position of the list called ListName
ListName.remove(x)	removes the first item x from the list called ListName
ListName.reserve(x)	reverses the elements of the list called ListName
ListName.sort()	sorts the orderable (only numbers or strings) items of the list called ListName

Example 1.7 Consider the list given as List1 = [2, 5, 'Onions', 'Truck', 50, 5, -3].
a) Remove the item named 'Truck' from the list.
b) Insert number 1234 after the 2nd item in the list.
c) Put the final list in the reversed order.

Solution. a) We can use **remove()** function to remove the first appeared specific value as follows:

```
>>> List1 = [2, 5, 'Onions', 'Truck', 50, 5, -3]
>>> List1.remove('Truck')
>>> print(List1)
[2, 5, 'Onions', 50, 5, -3]
>>>
```

b) We can use the **insert()** function to insert the number 1234 after the 2nd item as follows.

```
>>> List1.insert(2, 1234)
>>> print(List1)
[2, 5, 1234, 'Onions', 50, 5, -3]
>>>
```

c) Finally, we can use the **reverse()** function to put the items in reversed order as follows:

```
>>> List1.reverse()
>>> print(List1)
[-3, 5, 50, 'Onions', 1234, 5, 2]
>>>
```

◀

For sorting the items, **sort()** function can be used. But in using this function, the items should be all numbers, may be composed of mixed integers and float numbers, or strings.

1.5.5 Tuples

Tuples are yet another sequence of data types in Python. They are enclosed with parentheses () instead of square brackets. Tuples have structures. Their items cannot be changed once they are created.

```
>>> Tup = (1, 2, 5, 'Of', 'FC')
>>> type(Tup)
<class 'tuple'>
>>> len(Tup)
```

```
5
>>> Tup[3]
'Of'
>>>
```

1.5.6 Dictionaries

Dictionaries are another data type of pairs that holds keys corresponding to certain values. They are defined with curly brackets. Dictionaries appear like lists. However, lists are ordered sets of objects while dictionaries are unordered. Another important difference is that in dictionaries, items are reached by using their keys, not via their positions.

```
>>> Diction= {"Cars":"Cool","Doctor":"Antonio","City":"Dallas"}
>>> type(Diction)
<class 'dict'>
>>> Diction['Doctor']
'Antonio'
>>> Diction["City"] = "Austin"
>>> Diction["City"]
'Austin'
>>>
```

As can be above, each key corresponds to a value. Values can be changed through their keys.

Table 1.2: Some available functions used with the dictionaries

Function	**Explanation**
DictName.clear()	removes all the elements of dictionary named DictName
dict.fromkeys(seq,val)	creates a new dictionary with keys from seq and values from val
DictName.get(x)	finds the corresponding value of key x from dictionary named DictName
DictName.items()	returns a list of (key, value) pairs from dictionary named DictName
DictName.update(dictB)	adds key-value pairs from dictionary DictB to dictionary named DictName

Example 1.8 Consider the dictionary given as Dict1 = “Math”:”Calculus”, “Biology”:”Cell”, “Year”:2017 . Write a code to update this dictionary with “Age”:21

Solution. We can update the dictionary by using **update()** function as shown in the following.

```
>>> Dict1 = {"Math":"Calculus", "Biology":"Cell", "Year":2017}
>>> DictB = {"Age":21}
>>> Dict1.update(DictB)
>>> Dict1
{'Biology': 'Cell', 'Math': 'Calculus', 'Age': 21, 'Year': 2017}
>>>
```

◀

As it is seen above, after updating the dictionary, the items do not appear in order.

Example 1.9 A sequence is given as Seq1 = (‘first_name’, ‘last_name’, ‘Number’). Write a code to create a dictionary by using Seq1 as keys where 50 is the assigned value to all keys in the dictionary.

Solution. We can create the dictionary as follows.

```
>>> Seq1 = ('first_name', 'last_name', 'Number')
>>> NewDict = dict.fromkeys(Seq1,50)
>>> NewDict
{'last_name': 50, 'Number': 50, 'first_name': 50}
>>>
```

◄

1.6 Operators

Operators are the symbols or expressions that makes Python interpreter to infer results. There are arithmetic operators, relational or comparative operators, logical operators, assignment operators, bitwise operators and some other special operators used in Python.

1.6.1 Arithmetic Operators

Arithmetic operators are used to carry on mathematical calculations.

Table 1.3: Arithmetic Operators used in Python

Operator	Description	Example
+	Addition	6 + 3 = 9
-	Subtraction	6 - 3 = 3
*	Multiplication	6 * 3 = 18
/	Division	6 / 3 = 2
%	Modulo	6 % 3 = 0
**	Exponent	6 ** 3 = 216
//	Floor Division	6 // 3 = 2

In the table above, the Floor Division operator is a rounding operator. What it does is, after dividing, it rounds the result to the closest small integer. As an example, if you type ⋙ 24//5 and hit enter at the prompt, the result will be 4. When 24 is divided by 5, the result is 4.8; and if 4.8 is rounded to the closest small integer value, it equals 4.

1.6.2 Relational Operators

Relational operators are called comparative operators as well.2 operands are compared with the symbols given in the following table.

Table 1.4: Relational Operators used in Python

Operator	**Description**	**Example**
>	Greater than	6 >5
>=	Greater than or equal to	5 >= 5
<	Less that	2 <3
<=	Less than or equal to	3 <=5
==	Equal to	4 ==4
!=	Not equal to	1 !=5

If the case is correct, then True is returned from this comparison.

1.6.3 Logical Operators

There are three logical operators being used in Python.

Table 1.5: Logical Operators used in Python

Operator	Description	Example
and	True if both operands are true	A and B
or	True if one operand is true	A or B
not	True if operand is false	not A

1.6.4 Bitwise Operators

Bitwise operators result differently comparing to arithmetic operators. The operands behave like binary digits.

Table 1.6: Bitwise Operators used in Python

Operator	Description	Example
&	AND	12 & 7 =4
$\mid$	OR	12 $\mid$7 = 15
$\sim$	NOT	$\sim$ 12 = -13
$\wedge$	XOR	12$\wedge$7 =11
$\ll$	Right Shift	12 $\ll$ 7 = 1536
$\gg$	Left Shift	12 $\gg$ 7 = 0

In the figure above, 12 is equal to '1100' and 7 is equal to '0111' in binary format. If you apply & (and) operator to 1100 and 0111, the result is 0100 which is equal to 4 in decimal format. All other examples are calculated in similar ways.

1.6.5 Assignment Operators

Assignment operators are used to assign values to the variables.

Table 1.7: Assignment Operators used in Python

<table>
<tr><th>Operator</th><th>Sample Usage</th><th>Equivalent Usage</th></tr>
<tr><td>=</td><td>x = 9</td><td>x = 9</td></tr>
<tr><td>+=</td><td>x + = 9</td><td>x = x + 9</td></tr>
<tr><td>-=</td><td>x - = 9</td><td>x = x - 9</td></tr>
<tr><td>*=</td><td>x * = 9</td><td>x = x * 9</td></tr>
<tr><td>/=</td><td>x / = 9</td><td>x = x / 9</td></tr>
<tr><td>%=</td><td>x % = 9</td><td>x = x % 9</td></tr>
<tr><td>//=</td><td>x // = 9</td><td>x = x // 9</td></tr>
<tr><td>**=</td><td>x ** = 9</td><td>x = x ** 9</td></tr>
<tr><td>&=</td><td>x & = 9</td><td>x = x & 9</td></tr>
<tr><td>|=</td><td>x |= 9</td><td>x = x |9</td></tr>
<tr><td>∧ =</td><td>x ∧ = 9</td><td>x = x ∧ 9</td></tr>
<tr><td>≪ =</td><td>x ≪ =</td><td>x = x ≪ 9</td></tr>
<tr><td>≫ =</td><td>x ≫ = 9</td><td>x = x ≫ 9</td></tr>
</table>

1.6.6 Special Operators

There are some special operators being used in Python. These operators can be grouped as identity operators and membership operators. Identity operators are used to check whether two identity values are the same or not by using "is" and "is not". On the other hand, membership operators are used to find out whether or not a variable exists in a list, or in a group of items by using "in" and "not in".

Table 1.8: Special Operators used in Python

Operator	Sample Usage	Equivalent Usage
is	True if the values are same	x is y
is not	True if the values are not same	x is not y
in	True if value is in the list	2 in List
not in	True if value is not in the list	2 not in List

Example 1.10 Consider the variables given as Str1 = "Hello World", Num1 = 5, and Num2 = 5.
a) Write a code to check if "Hello" exists in the string Str1 by using special operator "in".
b) Write a code to check if Num1 and Num2 are equal by using special operator "is".

Solution. a) The following code may be entered at prompt to accomplish the given task.

```
>>> Str1 = "Hello World"
>>> print('Hello' in Str1)
True
>>>
```

b) The following code may be entered at prompt to accomplish the task.

```
>>> Num1 = 5
>>> Num2 = 5
>>> print(Num1 is Num2)
True
>>>
```

◄

1.7 Built-in Functions

Similar to other programming languages, there are ready to use functions called built-in functions in Python, too. These functions make the programmer's job much easier.

There are also functions defined by the user called user-defined functions. Construction of user-defined functions will be presented in Chapter 6.

Table 1.9: Built-in functions available in Python

abs()	enumerate()	issubclass()	range()
all()	eval()	iter()	repr()
any()	exec()	len()	reversed()
ascii()	filter()	list()	round()
bin()	float()	locals()	set()
bool()	format()	map()	setattr()
bytearray()	frozenset()	max()	slice()
bytes()	getattr()	memoryview()	sorted()
callable()	globals()	min()	staticmethod()
chr()	hasattr()	next()	str()
classmethod()	hash()	object()	sum()
compile()	help()	oct()	super()
complex()	hex()	open()	tuple()
delattr()	id()	ord()	type()
dict()	input()	pow()	vars()
dir()	int()	print()	zip()
divmod()	isinstance()	property()	__import__()

Any of these functions can be examined by using the help function at prompt. As an example, if you wonder what **bin()** function does, you can type ⋙ help(bin) and hit enter at prompt to see the following information.

```
>>> help(bin)
Help on built-in function bin in module builtins:
```

```
bin(number, /)
    Return the binary representation of an integer.

    >>> bin(2796202)
    '0b1010101010101010101010'

>>>
```

1.8 Formatting Output

We can set the format of the output while printing data on the screen. By using the "modulo" operator, an output can be shaped in the following manner.

```
>>> import math
>>> print("Pi is %10.4f" % math.pi)
Pi is     3.1416
>>> print("Pi is %2.7f" % math.pi)
Pi is 3.1415927
>>>
```

Above, the numbers after the modulo symbol set the spaces coming before the dot and digits after the dot as shown in π number above.

By using **format()** function, the same outputs can be printed on the screen in the following way.

```
>>> print("Pi is {:10.4f}".format(math.pi))
Pi is     3.1416
>>> print("Pi is {:2.7f}".format(math.pi))
Pi is 3.1415927
>>>
```

In the program above, curly brackets tell the Python interpreter that a data will be printed out in that position. We can use the **format()** function to print multiple data on the screen as follows, too.

```
>>> St1="Hello my friend"
>>> "{:s} : {:2.5f}".format(St1, math.pi)
'Hello my friend : 3.14159'
>>>
```

Table 1.10: Conversions used with modulo operator

Used Letter	**Meaning**
d	Signed integer in decimal format
i	Signed integer in decimal format
e	Floating point in exponential format
E	Signed integer in decimal format
f	Floating point in decimal format
F	Floating point in decimal format
c	Single character
s	String

1.9 PROBLEMS

1.1 Write a code to calculate the value of $y = sin(\frac{\pi}{3}) + \sqrt{5} + e^3$.

1.2 What are the differences between the functions *iskeyword()* and *isidentifier()*?

1.3 Which of the following or followings can be a variable name?

a) My_journey

b) What_wrong?_John

c) The yearis2018

d) 2000Yes

1.4 Given the formula F = m * a, write a script to calculate the value of a when m = 5 and F = 24.

1.5 Two strings are given as St1 = “Paris is in Europe” and S2 = “This Nice Continent”. Write a script to obtain “Europe Continent is Nice” by using S1 and S2.

1.6 If “Logical = bool(5¡4) or bool(10¿12)” is typed at prompt, what value will be assigned to the variable “Logical”?

1.7 A list given as List1 = [17, 61, ‘Table’]. Write a script that adds the number “1900” as a third item to List1.

1.8 A dictionary is given as Dict = “Name”:”Alex”, “Lesson”:”PE”, “Age”:40. Write a script that finds the corresponding value of the key “Age”.

1.9 If you type “(2**5)//6” at the prompt and hit the enter, what will the result be?

1.10 If you type “10%5” at the prompt and hit the enter, what will the result be?

1.11 After typing ⋙import math, and ⋙”:0.5f : :0.10f”.format (math.pi, math.pi) at the prompt, what will the output be?

Chapter 2

FOUNDATIONS OF PROGRAMMING

In this chapter, we will present the basics of programming with Python.

The topics such as algorithms, flowcharts, pseudocodes, scripts and Py files will be introduced and handled.

2.1 Introduction

A computer program is basically a set of instructions that tells computer what to do. In Python, for larger programs or codes, editor is preferred rather than typing everything at the prompt. The information we have learned so far was easy to execute and accomplish. Solving problems by just using the prompt, was enough for the examples we have done up to this point. We could use Python's editor to solve the same questions as well. However, for larger and more complex problems, it is recommended to keep your codes together organized in an editor file. Therefore, we will attempt to use the editor to type our codes for the rest of the problems throughout this book, as much as possible. As mentioned in the previous chapter, there are other Python editors that assist you in writing your codes, as well.

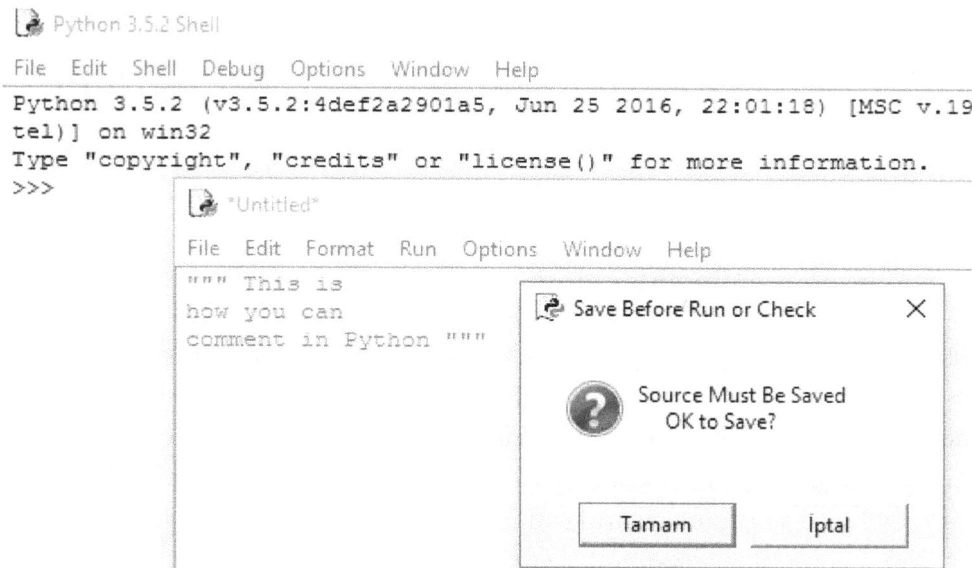

Figure 2.1: An outlook of a Warning pop-up window

If you type your codes in the editor and try to run it before saving, Python gives a warning to save it first. After saving your code, you can hit F5 over the editor, or follow the path Run → Run Modulo from the editor's menu.

It is not difficult to write complex, unorganized codes. After writing a program, if you need to look back to your code for some reason such as upgrading or rearranging the code, it might be difficult to understand what your code does in each line. Therefore, one of the primary concerns while creating a code is making them clear and easy to understand. To accomplish this, you can put some comments in the code as reminders after # symbol in a line. Comments are informative expressions to make the codes easy to understand. Python ignores whatever is written after the # symbol in a line. Putting a comment block is also possible by putting three quotation marks “”” to start a comment. It is necessary to put another set of three quotation marks to terminate the comment block as shown in the editor in Figure 2.1.

Another important factor for writing better codes is to use meaningful names for variables, or structures. That helps us remember our scripts easily for later times.

There exists other useful information related to writing better codes which is out of the scope of this book. For a basic understanding of the subject, we will keep it simple here.

2.2 Algorithms

Algorithm is a computational procedure which shows all the steps involved in solving a problem. Generally, an input (or a set of inputs) is taken and an output (or some outputs) is (are) produced. To solve a problem, the problem is separated into parts to examine and accomplish the pieces separately. In this way, the problem can be analyzed in a detailed manner. This method is often called a **top-down** approach. Sometimes, pieces are combined to get information about the entire system which yields more complex systems. We can build the system by analyzing and combining the pieces that we have gathered information about. This method is called **bottom-up** processing.

In either way, the purpose of the algorithms is to define a solution to a problem in some ways such as writing the solution with simple words, or showing the solution by using flowcharts.

2.3 Flowcharts and Pseudocodes

Both Pseudocodes and flowcharts are used to construct an algorithm of a computer program. While Pseudocodes are generally composed of words, flowcharts are represented by some simple shapes.

Pseudocodes are informal ways of describing the steps of the program to be written. It helps the programmers to plan and develop the ultimate algorithm for the computer program.

Flowchart is a graphical representation of the steps towards writing the program. Shapes along with diagrams are being used to explain the algorithm of the computer program.

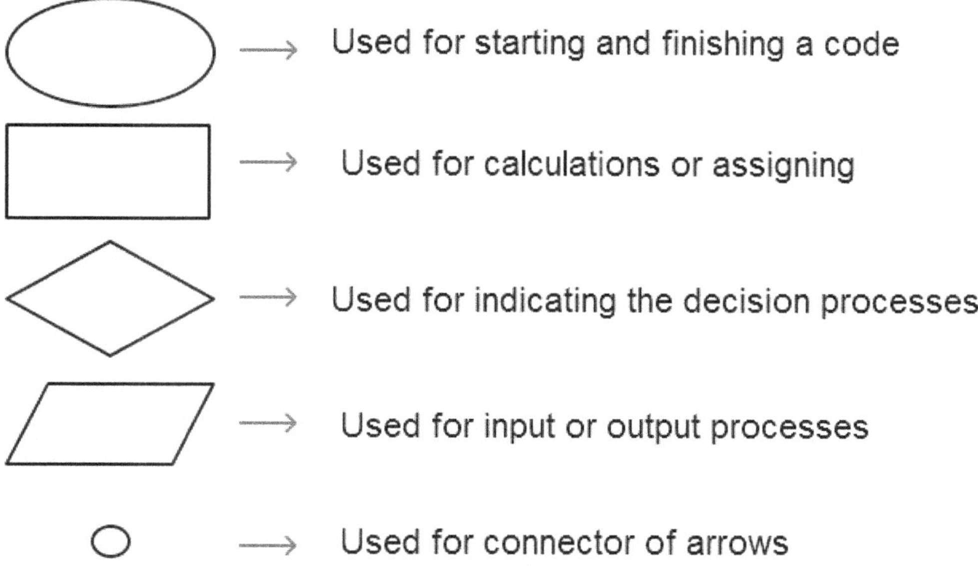

Figure 2.2: Commonly used flowchart symbols

Example 2.1 Construct a pseudocode and flowchart for an algorithm that calculates the area of a square. The length of one side of the square should be externally entered by the user.

Solution. For the pseudocode, we can write the steps of the algorithm as below.

1. Enter the side of the square, called B

2. Calculate the formula of the area of a square $Area = B^2$

3. Display the result, we got from the calculation, $Area$

Per the flowchart, we can represent the necessary steps as follows:

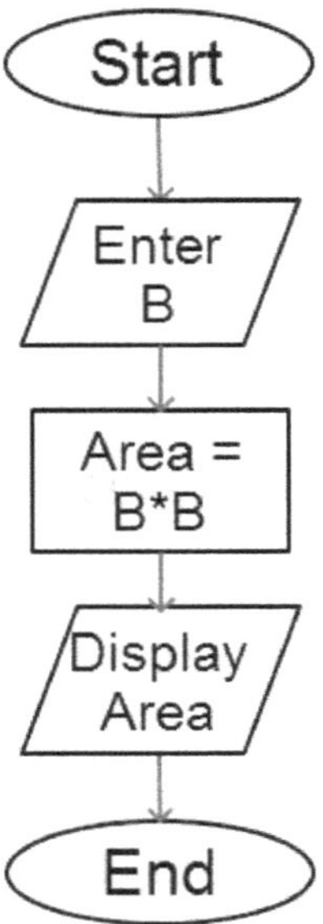

Figure 2.3: Flowchart of Example 2.1

2.4 Scripts and Py files

After an algorithm is determined to solve the problem, the code must be written to accomplish the given task. These codes can be written in Python editor and saved as a *.py file where * is substituted by the name you give your program. Thus, the codes written in Python are called Py files and these codes are called scripts or programs.

Example 2.2 Write the code of Example 2.1 to calculate the area of a square.

Solution. In this solution, we will use an important function, called **input()**. A data is passed to the computer by using input command. The default data type of input() function is the string. Therefore, if an integer or a float type is expected, then the data should be converted to int or float.

```
#Example 2.2
#This example calculates the area of a square
```

```
SideB = int(input("Please enter a side of the square :"))
Area = (SideB)**2
print("The Area of the square is :",Area)
```

Listing 2.1: Example2p2.py

Once you run the code, the following output will be obtained:

```
Please enter a side of the square :12
The Area of the square is : 144
```

◄

Above, the computer expects you to enter a number. Once the number is entered, it is convert-ed to an integer format and assigned to variable named *SideB*. Then the square of *SideB* is calculated and assigned to the variable named *Area*. Finally, the words between quotation marks are printed on first, and next to it, the value of Area is printed on the screen.

Example 2.3 Draw a flow chart of an algorithm and write the code which calculates the area and perimeter of a circle where the radius is entered by user.

Solution. The flowchart of the algorithm can be drawn as below.

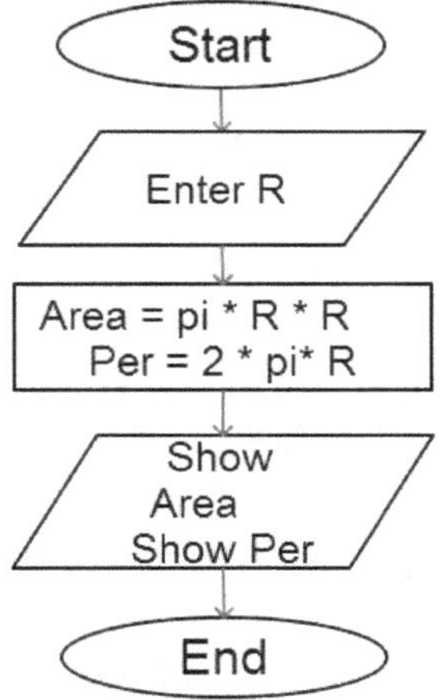

Figure 2.4: Flowchart of Example 2.3

The code can be written as follows:

```
1 #Example 2.3
2 #This example calculates the area and perimeter of a circle
3 import math
4 Ra = float(input("Please enter the Radius of the circle :\n"))
5 Area = math.pi * Ra**2
6 Per = 2*math.pi*Ra
7 print("The Area of the circle is :",Area)
8 print("The Perimeter of the circle is :",Per)
```

Listing 2.2: Example2p3.py

Once you run the code, the following output will be obtained:

```
Please enter the Radius of the circle :
6.5
The Area of the circle is : 132.73228961416876
The Perimeter of the circle is : 40.840704496667314
```

As it is seen from the code, we imported math module in order to use the value of π. There is "\n" is used in 4th line. This is one of the escape sequences used in Python. What it does is, after printing whatever comes before it, and then the cursor goes to the next line to continue from there.
That is the reason that, number 65 is entered in the next line at the output.

Table 2.1: Some of the used Escape Sequences in Python

Escape Sequence	Meaning
\‘	Single quote
\‘‘	Double quote
\\	Backslash
\n	New line
\t	Tab
\f	ASCII Form feed

Example 2.4 Write a flowchart of an algorithm that compares 20 with a number entered by the user. If the number that is entered is greater than 20, then the program must show "Number is greater than 20", otherwise, it should print "The entered number is less than or equal to 20" (Note: We will present how to write codes using if, if-else structures in the next chapter).

Solution. The flowchart of the algorithm can be drawn as below.

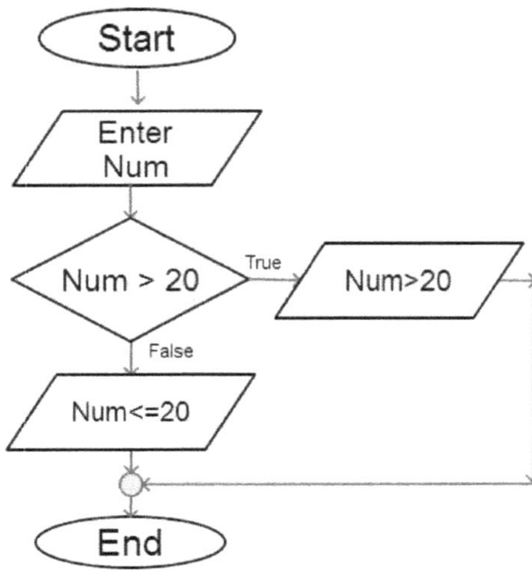

Figure 2.5: Flowchart of Example 2.4

2.5 PROBLEMS

2.1 Write the code and construct the flowchart of a program that takes 2 inputs as the shorter and longer sides of a rectangle, and print the area of the rectangle on the screen.
2.2 Create the flowchart of an algorithm that, for an entered number greater than 18, it prints "Yes you can take a driver's license", and otherwise "No driver license".
2.3 Think of an air pumping device that inflates tires. When the barometer of the pump reads 32, the device stops working. If it if less than 32, it keeps working and pumping air into the tire. Construct a flowchart for the algorithm of this device's operation.
2.4 Express the output of the following flowchart. What is the value printed on the screen?

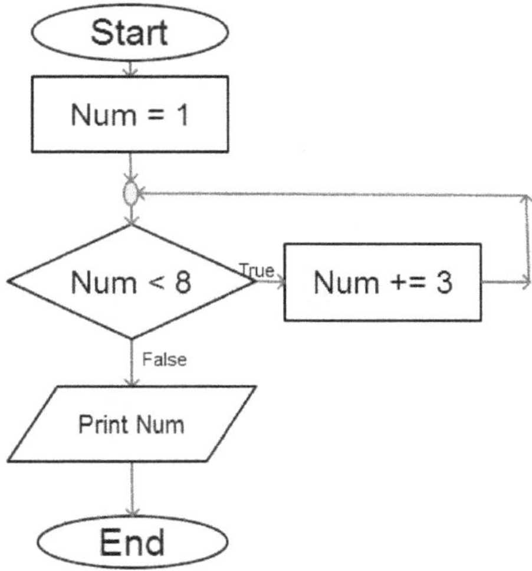

Figure 2.6: Flowchart of chapter problem 2.4

2.5 Express the output of the following flowchart. What is the value printed on the screen?

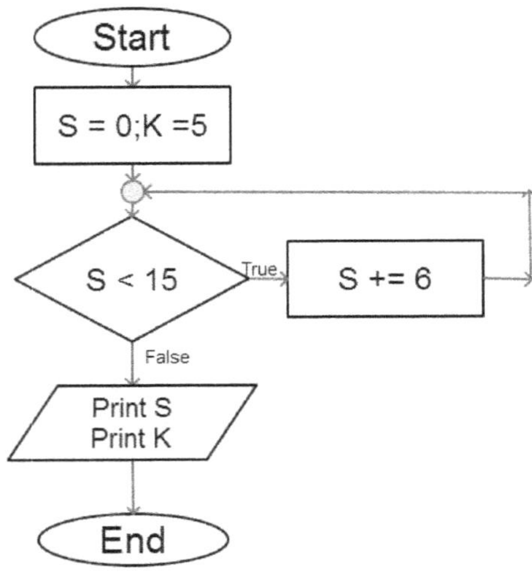

Figure 2.7: Flowchart of chapter problem 2.5

Chapter 3

LOGICAL FUNCTIONS AND SELECTION STRUCTURES

In this chapter we will present how to use **if**, **elif**, and **else** statements along with handling some error scenarios by using **try-except-finally** statements. In some cases, we need to select an option among a set of possible candidates. This selection may be made by using if-elif-else statements in Python.

Before continuing, we need to understand a rule related to indention.

Unlike some of other programming languages, in Python, when some keywords are used such as if, for, while, etc. neither the body part of these keywords are closed with the word “end” nor curly brackets are used to single out these blocks. Python interpreter needs to understand how to group these blocks, where they start and where they end. Therefore, when such statements are used including the “if” statement, indentation needs to be applied. Default indention amount is four spaces. Within our codes, we will use 4 spaces for all flow control blocks, too.

3.1 Single if-else Statement

If statements are always followed by a logical expression. However, in **else** statements, it is optional depending on the problem.

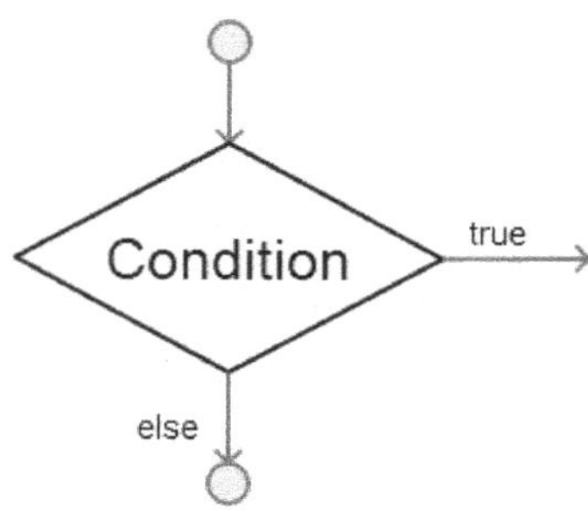

Figure 3.1: Flowchart of a single if-else statement

The usage of an if-else structure is given below.

```
if (Condition) :
        statement
else:
        statement
```

Example 3.1 Write a program which picks a pair of dice. If the sum of the rolled numbers are 10, then the program should print " Yes, you WON" on the screen. For all other cases, the computer should print "Try again" on the screen.

Solution. We will use random module to write the code.

```
#Example 3.1
#This example finds the sum of a pair of rolled dice
import random
Num1 = random.randrange(1,7)
Num2 = random.randint(1,6)
Sum = Num1 + Num2
if Sum == 10:
  print("Yes you WON")
else:
  print("Try again")
```

Listing 3.1: Example3p1.py

Once you run the code, the following output will be obtained.

```
Yes you WON
```

◀

In the above program, the functions **randrange()** and **randint()** are used via the random module. The difference between these functions is that the randrange() function picks numbers up to 7, excluding 7, while randint() function picks numbers up to 6, including 6.

Another point that needs to be considered is that you should put a colon at the end of each line of the "if" and "else" statements.

3.2 If-elif-else Statements

In this type, more than 1 option is checked. The flowchart of one **elif** with **if-else** statement can be drawn as following.

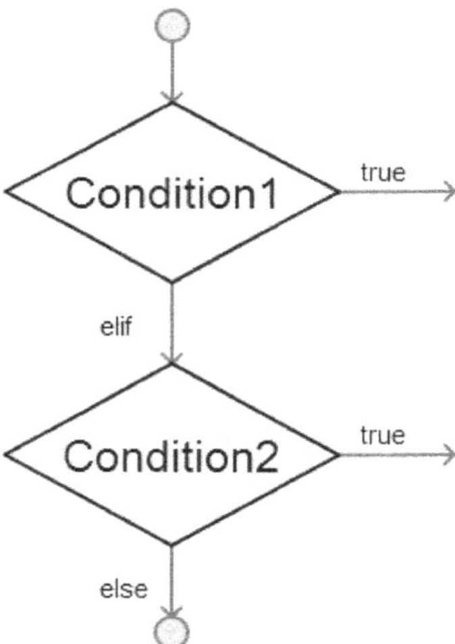

Figure 3.2: Flowchart of if-elif-else statement

As can be seen in the flowchart, if Condition1 is not satisfied, then Condition2 is checked. We may think of the statement elif as else if. If more than one elif statements are used, then every other condition is checked one by one with the other given conditions in the order.

Example 3.2 Write a program that requests the age of the user. If the entered age is less than 6, the code should print “No school yet” on the screen. If the age is between 6 and 14, it should print "Middle school". If the age is between 15 and 18, it should print "High school", and finally, if the age is between 19 and 24, it should print "University time". Otherwise, the program should print “You are ready for life” on the screen.

Solution. The following code may be used to accomplish the task.

```
#Example 3.2
#This example use if-elif-else statements
Age = int(input("Please enter your age :"))
if Age < 6:
    print("No school yet")
elif Age < 15:
    print("Middle school")
elif Age < 19:
    print("High school")
elif Age < 25:
    print("University time")
else:
    print("You are ready for the life")
```

Listing 3.2: Example3p2.py

Once you run the code, the computer expects a number. The number that is entered will be converted to integer format and assigned to the variable “age”. The variable “age” is compared to every condition. If one of the conditions is satisfied before the statement “else”, then the body part of that condition is executed. After running the code, we obtain the following output.

```
Please enter your age :25
You are ready for the life
```

◀

3.3 Logical Operators with if-else Statements

We might encounter some problems that we need to use logical operators with if statements.

Example 3.3 Write a program that requests the name and password of the user. If the name is "Alex" and the password is "2017 is nice", then the computer prints "Access is Granted". Otherwise, the computer should print "You are not the ONE" on the screen.

Solution. The following code may be used to accomplish the given task.

```
#Example 3.3
#This example uses logical and
UserName = 'Alex'
UserPassword = "2017 is nice"
User   = input("Your User Name :\n")
Password = input("Enter Password :\n")

if((UserName == User) and (UserPassword == Password)):
    print("Access is Granted")
else:
    print("You are not the ONE")
```

Listing 3.3: Example3p3.py

The following output will be obtained as you run the code.

```
Your User Name :
Alex
Enter Password :
2017 is nice
Access is Granted
```

◀

3.4 try-except-finally Statements

Up to this point, we have used nice inputs to run our codes. As an example, while it is expected to enter an integer value by the user, a string may be entered, and in such a case, an error may occur. Or some other types of error might occur due to some other reasons. To overcome such problems, **try-except** format is used. The main part that represents the aim is written after the "try" statement, and then the part that handles possible errors is written after the "except" statement. The word **finally** is used to execute the code written after that point for all possibilities.

Example 3.4 Write a program that requests the age of the user. Then, the age is printed on the screen. If an integer is not entered, then the code should handle the error with **except** statement.

Solution. The following code may be used to accomplish the given task.

```
#Example 3.4
#This example uses try-except
try:
    Age = int(input("Enter your Age :"))
    print("Your age is ", Age)

except ValueError:
    print("You should enter an integer")
```

Listing 3.4: Example3p4.py

In the code, a value error may occur for entering a string. And this situation can be handled by using "except ValueError" pair. Following is the output of the code above.

```
Enter your Age :Hello
You should enter an integer
```

◀

Sometimes, errors may occur while performing the calculations. Dividing a value by zero is such a kind.

Example 3.5 Write a program that requests your favorite number. The computer then prints the division of 100 by that favorite number. Use finally statement to print "Do not worry".

Solution. The following code may be used to accomplish the task.

```
#Example 3.5
#This example uses try-except-finally
try:
    FavNumber = int(input("Whats your favorite number: "))
    Divide = 100/ FavNumber
    print("100 / your number is : ", Divide)
except ZeroDivisionError:
    print("Do not pick ZERO")
finally:
        print("Do not worry")
```

Listing 3.5: Example3p5.py

The following output will result after running the code.

```
Whats your favorite number: 0
Do not pick ZERO
Do not worry
```

◀

Example 3.6 Write a program which calculates the roots of a quadratic equation of the form $ax^2 + bx + c = 0$. The coefficients a,b, and c should be entered by the user. If the roots are not real, then the code should give a value error.

Solution. The following code may be used to accomplish the task.

```
#Example 3.6
#This example find the roots of quadratic equation
import math
try:
    print("Please enter (a,b,c) the coefficients of quadratic equation")
    A = int(input("a :"))
    B = int(input("b :"))
    C = int(input("c :"))
    Delta = B**2-4*A*C
    x1 = (-B - math.sqrt(Delta))/(2*A)
    x2 = (-B + math.sqrt(Delta))/(2*A)
    print("The roots are {} and {}".format(x1,x2))
except ValueError:
```

```
    print("A value error occured")
```

Listing 3.6: Example3p6.py

The following output will be obtained after running the code.

```
Please enter (a,b,c) the coefficients of quadratic equation
a :12
b :5
c :3
A value error occured
```

◀

3.5 PROBLEMS

3.1 Write a code that rolls a pair of dice. If one of the numbers is 6 and the total sum of these two numbers is 10, then the computer prints "You are lucky" on the screen.
3.2 Write a program that requests the first and the last names of the user. If the first name is "Alex", or the last name is "Oliver", then the computer should print "You are my friend" on the screen. For all other options, it should print "Keep trying" on the screen.
3.3 Write a program that requests to enter a float number. If the number that is entered by the user is a string, then the code should request to enter it again by using the **except** statement.
3.4 Write a program that requests the user to enter a number. Then the program should calculate the absolute value of this number. If the data entered by the user is not a number, then the code should print a warning on the screen by using the "except ValueError" statement.
3.5 Write a program that asks your age. If the age is less than 18, the computer should print " No driver license". If the age is between 18 and 60, the program should print "You can apply for a driver license". If the age entered by the user is greater than 60, then the computer should print "You have a lot of experience" on the screen.
3.6 Draw the flowchart for the previous scenario in Problem 3.5.

Chapter 4

PROGRAM CONTROLS

In this chapter, we will discuss how to use the for loops, while loops, break-continue commands, and loops with Boolean expression.

Until a given condition is reached, loop control statements are used to execute a set of code. If the condition is not reached, the program keeps running in an indefinite loop. In that case, your computer may start to slow down and may freeze at some point.

The loops are sometimes called repetition structures, as well. Python has for loop and while loop structures as most programming languages do.

4.1 For loop

They are used to execute the codes inside the loop by going through a sequence of values. In general, for loops are used for a fixed number of times to accomplish a block of code.

Its usage can be summarized as follows.

```
for (variable) in (sequence):
        codes to be executed
```

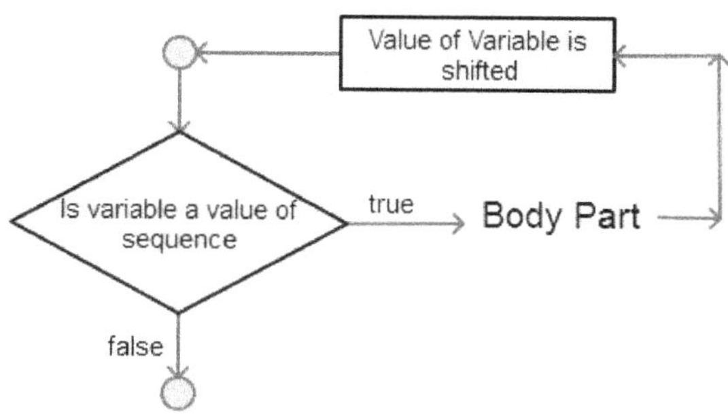

Figure 4.1: Flowchart of a for loop

Example 4.1 Write a code that calculates the square of numbers from 0 to 5.

Solution. The following code can be used to accomplish the given task.

```
#Example 4.1
#This example calculates the square of numbers
for i in range(6):
    print("The square of {} is {} ".format(i, i**2))
```

Listing 4.1: Example4p1.py

The following is the output of the code above.

```
The square of 0 is 0
The square of 1 is 1
The square of 2 is 4
The square of 3 is 9
The square of 4 is 16
The square of 5 is 25
```

◀

As can be seen above, **range()** function is used in the code.It is a very useful function in generating a sequence of values. It also has different usages, as well.

Table 4.1: Different usages of the function **range()**

Usage	Description
range(a+1)	generates integers from 0 to a
range(a,b+1)	generates integers from a to b
range(a,b+1, d)	generates integers from a to b going d by d

Example 4.2 Write a program that calculates the following series, which gives the value of ln(2).

$$\sum_{n=1}^{\infty} \frac{(-1)^{n+1}}{n} = 1 - \frac{1}{2} + \frac{1}{3} - \frac{1}{4} + ... = 0.693147$$

Solution. The loop approaches infinity. We need to set a final number instead of ∞. The higher the final number is picked, the more accurate the result will be. But, if the number is chosen too big, some machine errors might then be involved, which decrease the accuracy of your result. The following code may be written to accomplish the given task.

```
#Example 4.2
#This example calculates ln2
import math
Total = 0
for i in range(1,1000000):
     Number = (math.pow((-1),i+1))/i
     Total +=Number
print(Total)
```

Listing 4.2: Example4p2.py

In the foregoing program, 10^6 is chosen as the final value instead of infinity. The following is the output of this code.

```
0.6931476805602526
```

◀

Example 4.3 Write a program that prints a right triangle by using asterisks (*). The height is entered by the user. As an example, if the user enters 8, then one asterisk appears in the first row, two asterisks in the second row, three asterisks in the third row, and so on.

Solution. The following code can be used to accomplish the task.

```
#Example 4.3
#This example prints out right triangle by using asterisks
Height = int(input("What is the height of the right triangle ? "))
for i in range(1,Height+1):
    print("*"*i)
```

Listing 4.3: Example4p3.py

The following is the output of the code above.

```
What is the height of the right triangle ? 7
*
**
***
****
*****
******
*******
```

As it is seen, the number of asterisks is increased when the asterisk is multiplied by a higher number. ◀

4.2 While loop

In some cases, number of iterations is not known in the loop. Or holding a loop is necessary to reach a certain value. In such cases, while loop should be preferred. The structure of this loop is shown below.

```
while (condition):
        body part
```

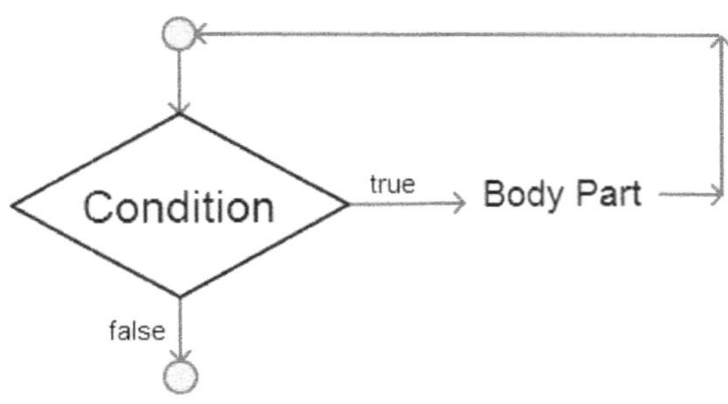

Figure 4.2: Flowchart of a while loop

Example 4.4 Write a code that requests the user to enter a number. The program is required to keep asking a number until a negative number is entered.

Solution. The following code can be used to accomplish the task.

```
#Example 4.4
#This example keeps asking to enter a negative number
Number = int(input("Please enter a negative number "))
while Number > 0 :
    print("You should enter a negative number to quit")
    Number = int(input("Please enter a negative number "))
print("Thank you for entering ", Number)
```

Listing 4.4: Example4p4.py

The following is the output of the given code.

```
Please enter a negative number 10
You should enter a negative number to quit
Please enter a negative number 4
You should enter a negative number to quit
Please enter a negative number -6
Thank you for entering  -6
```

◀

Example 4.5 Write a code that calculates the factorial of a number entered by the user.

Solution. The following code can be used to accomplish the task.

```
#Example 4.5
#This example calculates the factorial of entered number
Factorial = 1
Counter = 1
Number = int(input("Enter a number to calculate its factorial: "))
if (Number < 1) :
    print("You should enter a positive integer")
else:
    while (Counter <= Number):
        Factorial *= Counter
        Counter += 1
    print("Factorial of {} is {} ".format(Number, Factorial))
```

Listing 4.5: Example4p5.py

The following is the output of the code above.

```
Enter a number to calculate its factorial: 6
Factorial of 6 is 720
```

◀

4.3 Break-Continue Statements

In a **for** or **while** loop, when the **break** statement is read by the interpreter, it terminates and gets out of the closest loop.

Example 4.6 Write a code that requests the user to enter a positive integer. Then, the program should calculate the Fibonacci numbers up to that number.

Solution. The following code can be used to accomplish the task.

```
#Example 4.6
#This example calculates the Fibonacci numbers
Fibo = [1,1]
Number = int(input("Enter a number : "))
```

```
while True:
    if (Number<1):
        print("The number should be positive")
    else:
        for i in range(2, Number):
            NewValue = Fibo[i-1] + Fibo[i-2]
            Fibo.append(NewValue)
        print(Fibo)
        break
```

Listing 4.6: Example4p6.py

Within the code, the condition for the while loop is True, which means that it keeps running if it is not terminated, or broken out. If the number entered by the user is positive, then the computer starts calculating numbers and assigns them to the variable named *NewValue*. Each time, these created values are appended to the list which holds all Fibonacci numbers. Once all numbers are calculated, by using the **break** statement, while loop is terminated and numbers are printed on the screen.

```
Enter a number : 10
[1, 1, 2, 3, 5, 8, 13, 21, 34, 55]
```

◀

Example 4.7 Write a program that requests the name and password of the user. If the user- name and password match as "Alexander" and "07Nicky" respectively, the computer then prints "Welcome Alexander" on the screen. If one of these entries does not match, then the program asks the user to change the one that does not match. In order to close the program, both data should be entered correctly.

Solution. The following code can be used to accomplish the task.

```
#Example 4.7
#This example asks for user name and password
UserName = "Alexander"
UserPassword = "07Nicky"
while True:
    User = input("Please Enter User Name : ")
    Password = input("Please Enter Password : ")
```

```
    if ((User == UserName) and (Password == UserPassword)):
        print("Welcome ", User)
        break
    elif((User == UserName) and (Password != UserPassword)):
        print("Forgot your Password?")
        print("Dou you want to change your password(Y for Yes/ N for No)")
        Answer = input()
        if (Answer == 'Y'):
            NewPassword = input("Enter your new password : ")
            print("Please wait....")
            UserPassword = NewPassword
            print("Password changed successfully.")
    elif((User != UserName) and (Password == UserPassword)):
        print("Forgot your User Name?")
        print("Dou you want to change your username?(Y for Yes/ N for No)")
        Answer = input()
        if (Answer == 'Y'):
            NewUserName = input("Enter your new username : ")
            print("Please wait....")
            UserName = NewUserName
            print("User name changed successfully.")
```

Listing 4.7: Example4p7.py

Once the user name and password match, the loop is terminated by **break** statement. Output of this code is given in the following.

```
Please Enter User Name : Alexander
Please Enter Password : 07nicky
Forgot your Password?
Dou you want to change your password(Y for Yes/ N for No)
Y
Enter your new password : 08Nicky
Please wait....
Password changed successfully.
Please Enter User Name : Alexander
Please Enter Password : 08Nickey
Forgot your Password?
```

```
Dou you want to change your password(Y for Yes/ N for No)
N
Please Enter User Name : Alexander
Please Enter Password : 08Nicky
Welcome  Alexander
```

◀

In some cases, using **continue** statement makes the job easier as shown in the following example.

Example 4.8 Write a program that prints the numbers between 1 and 10 excluding numbers from a list given as List = [2, 3, 8, 9].

Solution. The following code can be used to accomplish the task.

```
#Example 4.8
#This example about using continue
MyList = [2, 3, 8, 9]
print("You can just use the following numbers ")
for i in range(1,11):
    if i in MyList:
        continue
    print(i)
```

Listing 4.8: Example4p8.py

Once the user name and password match, the loop is terminated by break statement.

```
You can just use the following numbers
1
4
5
6
7
10
```

As it is seen, when **continue** is in progress, codes come after **continue** is omitted. ◀

Example 4.9 Write a program that calculates the Euler number up to a given tolerance number as $Tol = 0.0001$ where it can be calculated by

$$E = \sum_{n=0}^{\infty}(\frac{1}{n!})$$

Solution. The following code can be used to accomplish the task.

```
#Example 4.9
#This example calculates Euler number
import math
Total = 1
Count = 1
Eul = 2.71828182
Tolerance = 0.0001

while True:
    Number = (1/math.factorial(Count))
    Total += Number
    if (math.fabs(Eul-Total) < Tolerance):
        break
    Count += 1
print("When n = {} , Euler is {}".format(Count, Total))
```

Listing 4.9: Example4p9.py

The output for the code is shown below.

```
When n = 7 , Euler is 2.7182539682539684
```

◀

As a final example to this chapter, we will write the code of a "guess the number" game.

Example 4.10 Write a program that guides the user to guess a number between 1 and 100 picked by the computer. The program should guide the user like "Go Down" or "Go up" depending on the number entered by the player. The code should display the number of trials on the screen as well.

Solution. The following code can be used to accomplish the task.

```
#Example 4.10
#This example guess picked number
import random
PickedNumber = random.randint(1,100)
Counter = 1
Gues = int(input('Please enter your Guess : '))
while True:
    if (Gues == PickedNumber):
        print("Congratulations. You got it in your {} th try".format(Counter
    ))
        break
    elif (Gues > PickedNumber):
        print("Go DOWN...")
        Gues = int(input("Please Enter your New Guess : "))
    else:
        print("Go UP...")
        Gues = int(input("Please Enter your New Guess : "))
    Counter += 1
```

Listing 4.10: Example4p10.py

A sample output for the code is shown below.

```
Please enter your Guess : 50
Go UP...
Please Enter your New Guess : 75
Go UP...
Please Enter your New Guess : 90
Go DOWN...
Please Enter your New Guess : 80
Go DOWN...
Please Enter your New Guess : 78
Congratulations. You got it in your 5 th try
```

◀

4.4 PROBLEMS

4.1 Write a program that requests the user to enter an integer. Then, the program calculates the sum of the squares of integers from 1 up to that number. The sum should be printed on the screen.

4.2 Write a program that prints a rectangle by using asterisks (*) on the screen. The length and width are to be entered by the user.

4.3 Write a program to calculate the value of π using the following series
$\pi = 4(1 - \frac{1}{3} + \frac{1}{5} - \frac{1}{7} + \frac{1}{9} - ...)$

4.4 Write a program that calculates the sum of 3rd powers of the numbers from 1 to 10.

4.5 Write a program that calculates the e^3 by using the following series up to a given tolerance number $Tolerance = 0.001$. The real value of e^3 is 20.0855369.

$$e^3 = \sum_{n=0}^{\infty}(\frac{3^n}{n!})$$

4.6 Write a code that requests the user to enter a negative number. The program should keep asking until a negative number is entered.

4.7 Write a program that prints the numbers between 1 and 20 excluding the numbers from a list given as List $= [1, 5, 6, 15, 16]$.

4.8 Write a program that rolls a pair of dice. The program should print the sum of the rolled numbers on the screen automatically every time until the sum is obtained to be 10.

Chapter 5

CORE DATA TYPES

Once the modules are imported and used, some other data types may appear in Python. By core data types, we refer to the data types that come with the Python interpreter without any need for extra modules, which are also called standard data types.

In chapter 1, standard data types were already introduced. In this chapter, we will elaborate on the ones that are widely used in most applications and sometimes may be difficult for the users to understand. These include, but are not limited to, strings, lists, and dictionaries.

5.1 Strings

Strings are one the most popular types in Python. They can be easily defined by putting them between single quotes, or double quotes.

To play with the letters, numbers or symbols as strings in greater detail, standard ASCII table can be used. At this point, two im-portant built-in functions emerge, namely, **chr()** and **ord()**.

By using chr() function, we can find the corresponding number of a character used in ASCII table. Similarly, by using ord() function, we can find the character corresponding to a number.

ASCII TABLE

Dec	Char	Dec	Char	Dec	Char	Dec	Char	Dec	Char
32		52	4	72	H	92	\	112	p
33	!	53	5	73	I	93	]	113	q
34	"	54	6	74	J	94	^	114	r
35	#	55	7	75	K	95	_	115	s
36	$	56	8	76	L	96	`	116	t
37	%	57	9	77	M	97	a	117	u
38	&	58	:	78	N	98	b	118	v
39	'	59	;	79	O	99	c	119	w
40	(	60	<	80	P	100	d	120	x
41	)	61	=	81	Q	101	e	121	y
42	*	62	>	82	R	102	f	122	z
43	+	63	?	83	S	103	g	123	{
44	,	64	@	84	T	104	h	124	|
45	-	65	A	85	U	105	i	125	}
46	.	66	B	86	V	106	j	126	~
47	/	67	C	87	W	107	k	127	DEL
48	0	68	D	88	X	108	l		
49	1	69	E	89	Y	109	m		
50	2	70	F	90	Z	110	n		
51	3	71	G	91	[	111	o		

Figure 5.1: Standard ASCII Table

Example 5.1 Write a program that finds the corresponding numbers of the string "Street No: 61" from the ASCII table.

Solution. The following code can be used to accomplish the given task.

```
#Example 5.1
#This example uses ord and str functions
String1 = "Street No: 61"
Correspond = ""

for char in String1:
    Correspond += str(ord(char)) + " "
#Double quotation marks above put a space between the values
print(Correspond)
```

Listing 5.1: Example5p1.py

Once the code is run, the following output will be obtained.

```
83 116 114 101 101 116 32 78 111 58 32 54 49
```

As can be seen from the output, these are the numbers corresponding to every character of "Street No: 61" from the ASCII table. ◀

Example 5.2 Write a program that splits the string "Bright Color for John 2017" into its words and puts these words in a list. Then, the first three characters of these words should be printed on the screen.

Solution. The following code may be used to accomplish the task.

```
#Example 5.2
#This example uses split() function
String = "Bright Color for John 2017"
Separate = String.split()
print("String is separates as a list :\n",Separate)
for char in Separate:
    print(char[:3], end=" ")#this puts strings in a row with a
    # space between them
```

Listing 5.2: Example5p2.py

Once the code is run, the following output will be obtained.

```
String is separates as a list :
 ['Bright', 'Color', 'for', 'John', '2017']
Bri Col for Joh 201
```

◀

Example 5.3 A message is given as "How are you doing there? No problem here 07". Write a program that encrypts this message and prints the encrypted message on the screen. Then, the message should be decrypted back and printed on the screen.

Solution. The following code can be used to accomplish the task.

```
#Example 5.3
#This example encrypts and decrypts a message
MyMessage = "How are you doing there? No problem here 07"
Key = 2 # each character is shifted 2 times
EncryptedMessage = ""
DecryptedMessage = ""
#Encryption starts here
```

```
for char in MyMessage:
    Shift = chr(ord(char) + Key)
    EncryptedMessage += Shift
print("Encrypted message is :\n", EncryptedMessage)
#Decryption starts here
for char in EncryptedMessage:
    Shift = chr(ord(char) - Key)
    DecryptedMessage += Shift
print("Decrypted message is :\n", DecryptedMessage)
```

Listing 5.3: Example5p3.py

As it is seen above, each character is shifted right by the key size, which is 2 for this encryption. For the decryption process, shifting is applied back to the left.

Once the program is run, the following output will be obtained.

```
Encrypted message is :
 Jqy"ctg"{qw"fqkpi"vjgtgA"Pq"rtqdngo"jgtg"29
Decrypted message is :
 How are you doing there? No problem here 07
```

◀

5.2 Lists

Lists can only have numbers or mixtures of numbers and characters. We can create multi-dimensional arrays with lists, as well.

Example 5.4 Write a program that creates a list having 10 elements. The elements should be picked randomly between 0 and 100. Then, the code should sort the elements and print them on the screen.

Solution. The following code can be used to accomplish the task.

```
#Example 5.4
#This example creates and sorts a list having 10 elements
import random

MyList = []
```

```
for i in range(10):
    MyList.append(random.randrange(0, 101))
print("Unsorted list : ", MyList)
MyList.sort() # list is sorted here
print("Sorted list   : ", MyList)
```

Listing 5.4: Example5p4.py

Once the program is run, the following output will be obtained.

```
Unsorted list :  [27, 21, 47, 19, 10, 0, 18, 14, 22, 41]
Sorted list   :  [0, 10, 14, 18, 19, 21, 22, 27, 41, 47]
```

◀

Example 5.5 Write a program that has two lists. First list should have numbers from 0 to 5 with 6 elements. The second list consists of "Alex, TX, Ringo, 2017". The code should combine these lists and print the elements on the screen.

Solution. The following code can be used to accomplish the task.

```
#Example 5.5
#This example combine 2 lists
FirstList = list(range(6))
SecondList = ['Alex', 'TX', 'Ringo', 2017]
FinalList = FirstList + SecondList
print(FinalList)
```

Listing 5.5: Example5p5.py

Once the program is run, the following output will be obtained.

```
[0, 1, 2, 3, 4, 5, 'Alex', 'TX', 'Ringo', 2017]
```

◀

Example 5.6 Write a program that creates a 10 by 10 array

Solution. The following code may be used to accomplish the task.

```
#Example 5.6
#This example creates a 10 by 10 array
Listing = range(10)
MyArray =  [[0] * 10 for i in range(10)]

for i in range(10):
    for k in range(10):
        MyArray[i][k] = i*k
        print(MyArray[i][k], end=",")
    print()
```

Listing 5.6: Example5p6.py

The code creates a list with 10 elements. Each element also has 10 elements in it. As the last **print()** function is executed, all these 10 elements are printed in a row. Once the program is run, the following output will be obtained.

```
0,0,0,0,0,0,0,0,0,0,
0,1,2,3,4,5,6,7,8,9,
0,2,4,6,8,10,12,14,16,18,
0,3,6,9,12,15,18,21,24,27,
0,4,8,12,16,20,24,28,32,36,
0,5,10,15,20,25,30,35,40,45,
0,6,12,18,24,30,36,42,48,54,
0,7,14,21,28,35,42,49,56,63,
0,8,16,24,32,40,48,56,64,72,
0,9,18,27,36,45,54,63,72,81,
```

As it is seen above, matrices can be created in this way. ◄

5.3 Dictionaries

A dictionary pairs the keys with the values. We can change a data in a dictionary after creating it as well.

Example 5.7 A set of data is given as 'FirstItem':20, 'SecondItem':1, ThirdItem':100, FourthItem':50, 'LastItem':5. Write a program to sort these elements.

Solution. The following code may be used to accomplish the given task.

```
#Example 5.7
#This example sorts the elements
MyData = {'FirstItem':20,
          'SecondItem':1,
          'ThirdItem':100,
          'FourthItem':50,
          'LastItem':5}
Sorting1 = zip(MyData.values(), MyData.keys())
Sorting2 = zip(MyData.keys() , MyData.values())
print(sorted(Sorting1))
print(sorted(Sorting2))
```

Listing 5.7: Example5p7.py

zip() function aggregates the elements from the sets. And, by using **sort()** function, the data is sorted. Once the program is run, the following output is obtained.

```
[(1, 'SecondItem'), (5, 'LastItem'), (20, 'FirstItem'),
(50, 'FourthItem'), (100, 'ThirdItem')]
[('FirstItem', 20), ('FourthItem', 50), ('LastItem', 5),
('SecondItem', 1), ('ThirdItem', 100)]
```

◄

Example 5.8 A set of data given as "Name":"Clint", "Address":"Hotel", "Number":9001. Write a code to change the value corresponding to "Number" to be 2020.

Solution. The following code can be used to accomplish the task.

```
#Example 5.8
#This example changes the value of a key
MyDiction = {"Name":"Clint", "Address":"Hotel", "Number":9001}
print("My data before changing is :\n", MyDiction)
MyDiction["Number"] = 2020
print("My data after changing is :\n", MyDiction)
```

Listing 5.8: Example5p8.py

Once the program is run, the following output will be obtained.

```
My data before changing is :
 {'Number': 9001, 'Name': 'Clint', 'Address': 'Hotel'}
My data after changing is :
 {'Number': 2020, 'Name': 'Clint', 'Address': 'Hotel'}
```

◀

5.4 PROBLEMS

5.1 Write a program that finds the corresponding numbers of the string "2017 is a nice year" from ASCII table.

5.2 Write a program that splits the string "Was born in San Antonio" into its words and puts these words in a list. Then, the first two characters of these words should be printed on the screen.

5.3 A set of dictionary data is given as 'LastItem':50, 'Item':1, 'List':60, 'Another':50. Write a program to sort these elements.

5.4 A message is given as "I will be working this summer". Write a program that encrypts this message and prints the encrypted message on the screen. Then, the message should be decrypted back and printed on the screen, as well.

5.5 Write a program that has two lists. First list should have numbers from 10 to 20 with 10 elements. The second list consists of "Tomato, CA, Diego, 2100". The code should combine the lists and print the elements on the screen.

Chapter 6

USER-DEFINED FUNCTIONS

There are some functions that are ready to use with the Python interpreter. These functions are called built-in functions. The user can also define functions for specific purposes, as well. These functions are called user-defined functions.

6.1 Defining a Function

To define a function, there is a specific structure to follow.

```
def NameofFunction(OptionalVar):
            body part
```

In the structure above, **def** is followed by the function name. It is mandatory to use the parentheses. And the parentheses must be followed by a colon. Inside the parentheses, there may or may not be a variable or variables depending on the function to be defined. Some of the reasons defining a function can be explained as follows.

In larger programs, it is preferred to divide the whole code into several parts by using user defined functions to make the program easy to understand, to maintain it well for future purposes, and to fix the errors if there occurs any.

Example 6.1 In a program, define two functions. The first one prints "Hello World !!" on the screen, while other one accepts a number and prints it on the screen.

Solution. The following code can be used to accomplish the task.

```
#Example 6.1
#This code defines two functions
def Hello():
    print("Hello World !!!\n")
def Age(numb):
    print("Your number is ",numb)

Hello()
Age(40)
```

Listing 6.1: Example6p1.py

The **Hello()** function does not accept any value while a value of 40 is passed to the **Age()** function. Once the program is run, the following output will be obtained.

```
Hello World !!!n
Your number is  40
```

◄

The variables defined inside a function are called **local** variables while the variables defined outside the functions are called **global** variables. Local variables are not available if their values are used outside the functions.

Example 6.2 Write a program that shows the differences between using a global variable inside and outside the function.

Solution. The following code may be used to accomplish the given task.

```
#Example 6.2
#This code uses local and global variables.
Numb1 = 61 #this is global variable
def MyFunction():
    Numb1 = 55 #this is local variable
    print("My Global variable inside a function is : ", Numb1)
MyFunction()
print("My Global variable outside a function is : ", Numb1)
print("******** Using Another function ***********")
Numb2 = 34 #this is global variable
def MySecondFunction():
    global Numb2 # this is defined as global
```

```
    Numb2 = 6 #this value is global anymore
    print("My Global variable inside a function is : ", Numb2)
MySecondFunction()
print("My Global variable outside a function is : ", Numb2)
```

Listing 6.2: Example6p2.py

Once the program runs, the following output will be obtained.

```
My Global variable inside a function is :  55
My Global variable outside a function is :  61
******** Using Another function ***********
My Global variable inside a function is :  6
My Global variable outside a function is :  6
```

◀

Example 6.3 Write a program that downloads an image from a **url** link provided by the user. In this example, you need to import the "urllib.request" module.

Solution. The following code may be used to accomplish the task.

```
#Example 6.3
#This example defines a function which
# downloads an image over the web.
import urllib.request
def ImageOverWeb(url):
    NewName = "Handsome.jpg"
    urllib.request.urlretrieve(url, NewName)# save it
ImageOverWeb("http://www.teachmatlab.com/resim.jpg")
```

Listing 6.3: Example6p3.py

There should be the specified image in the URL address in order to run the code correctly. Once the code runs, the image will be downloaded and saved to the directory as "Handsome.jpg". ◀

Example 6.4 Define a function that takes 3 values for a triangle to calculate its perimeter. If no value is passed to the function, the function should use the default values for calculation.

Solution. The following code can be used to accomplish the task.

```
#Example 6.4
#This example shows passing values
def PerimeterOfTriangle(a=5, b=6, c=7):
    Perimeter = a + b + c
    print("Perimeter for a ={}, b ={}, c ={} is ={}".
          format(a, b, c, Perimeter))

PerimeterOfTriangle(10,15,20)#passes 3 values in order
PerimeterOfTriangle() # no values
PerimeterOfTriangle(b=20,c=30,a=40)#passes values in a mixed order
```

Listing 6.4: Example6p4.py

In the program above, if no value is passed to the function, then the default values are used. Values can be passed in a mixed order by using their variable names, as well. Once the program runs, the following output will be obtained.

```
Perimeter for a =10, b =15, c =20 is =45
Perimeter for a =5, b =6, c =7 is =18
Perimeter for a =40, b =20, c =30 is =90
```

◀

Example 6.5 Define a function that adds all the passed values up and prints the result on the screen, even if the number of passed values is not known.

Solution. The following code can be used to accomplish the task.

```
#Example 6.5
#This code accepts flexible number of arguments
def AddNumbers(*args):
    Adding = 0
    for i in args:
        Adding += i
    print("Result of Adding all numbers is ", Adding)
AddNumbers()
AddNumbers(5)
AddNumbers(3, 5, 10)
```

```
AddNumbers(20, 30, 40, 60, 100)
```

Listing 6.5: Example6p5.py

While defining the function, "*args" has to be used inside the parentheses. Once the program runs, the following output will be obtained.

```
Result of Adding all numbers is  0
Result of Adding all numbers is  5
Result of Adding all numbers is  18
Result of Adding all numbers is  250
```

◀

6.2 Creating a Module

Modules involve functions defined within them. We may create a Python file and define some functions in it. Then, by importing our file to a program, we can use the defined functions from that file.

Example 6.6 Write a program that calls a function named "Greetings" from the module "Example6p6.py", where the content of the module "Example6p6.py" is given below.

```
#Example 6.6
#This file has 3 defined functions in it
def Greetings(name):
    print("Hello. How are you ", name)

def AddNumbers(*args):
    Adding = 0
    for i in args:
        Adding += i
    print(Adding)

def WhatIsWrong():
    print("What is wrong with that !!")
```

Listing 6.6: Example6p6.py

Solution. First, we need to import the name of the module and then call the function. The following code may be used to accomplish the task.

```
#Example 6.6
#This file calls a function from module named Example6p6.py
import Example6p6
Example6p6.Greetings("Irfan")
```

Listing 6.7: Example6p7.py

Once the program runs, the following output will be obtained.

```
Hello. How are you  Irfan
```

◀

6.3 PROBLEMS

6.1 Define a function that prints "Hello Folks!!" on the screen when it is called by a program. The program should call the function twice.

6.2 Write a program that calls a function to add 5 passed numbers up and print the result on the screen.

6.3 Write a program that downloads an image from a passed url link.

6.4 Write a program that has a function which takes 2 values to calculate the perimeter and area of a rectangle. If no value is passed to the function, the function should use default values for calculation. In the program, call the function twice, and use it with and without given values.

6.5 Write a program that has a function defined in it. The function should multiply all the entered values and print the result on the screen even if the number of passed values is not known.

Chapter 7

FILE INPUT AND OUTPUT

7.1 Introduction

There are numerous types of data formats in today's digital era. Working with text files, word, excel, image files, and any other data files is sometimes inevitable depending on the task. Therefore, like some other important programming languages, Python offers important functions to work with files, too. In this chapter, we will discuss how to interact with text files.

Table 7.1: Some of the available modes in opening files

Modes	Description
r	Opens a file for reading only
r+	Opens a file for both reading and writing
w	Opens a file for writing only, overwrites if file exists, creates a file otherwise
w+	Opens a file for both writing and reading
a	Opens a file for appending

Example 7.1 Write a program that reads the file "Trying.txt" from the directory. The

program will print the number of lines and the content on the screen.

Solution. The following code can be used to accomplish the task.

```
#Example 7.1
#This example opens a file for reading
f = open('Trying.txt','r')
Text = f.readlines() #this reads all the lines
print("The file has {} lines".format(len(Text)))
print("The content of the file is :")
print(Text)
f.close()
```

Listing 7.1: Example7p1.py

In the code, "list(f)" command can be used instead of the "f.readlines()" command. The file is closed with the **close()** function. Once the program runs, the following output will be obtained.

```
The file has 3 lines
The content of the file is :
['Hello!! This is\n', 'just a try for \n', 'a nice purpose.']
```

◄

In the output, "\n" means that the line is finished at that point and the file continues from the next line.

Example 7.2 Write a program that reads the same file as in Example 7.1. Then, the program will ignore the first 15 characters in the file, and will read the next 11 characters right after that.

Solution. The following code can be used to accomplish the task.

```
#Example 7.2
#This example reads some data from a file
f = open('Trying.txt','r')
f.seek(15) #go 15 character forward
Text = f.read(11) # then read 11 character
print(Text)
```

Listing 7.2: Example7p2.py

Once the program runs, the following output will be obtained.

```
just a try
```

◀

Example 7.3 Write a program that reads the same file as in Example 7.1. Then add "I like this text" to the end of the original text.

Solution. The following code can be used to accomplish the task.

```
#Example 7.3
#This example adds some text at the end of file
f = open('Trying.txt','r+')
Text = f.readlines() #this reads all the lines
print("Before adding text:\n", Text)
NewText = "I like this text"
f.writelines(NewText)
f.seek(0) # go to beginning of file
print("After adding text:\n", list(f))
```

Listing 7.3: Example7p3.py

Once the program runs, the following output will be obtained.

```
Before adding text:
 ['Hello!! This is\n', 'just a try for \n', 'a nice purpose.\n']
After adding text:
 ['Hello!! This is\n', 'just a try for \n', 'a nice purpose.\n',
 'I like this text']
```

◀

Example 7.4 Write a program that reads the same file as in the previous example. Then add "Python is coming !!!" to the beginning of the second line.

Solution. The following code can be used to accomplish the task.

```
#Example 7.4
#This example inserts a string into a line
with open('Trying.txt','r+') as fil:
    NewText = "Python is coming !!!"
    Text = fil.readlines()
    print("Before inserting the text:\n", Text)
    fil.seek(0)
    Text.insert(1, NewText)
    fil.writelines(Text)
    fil.seek(0)
    print("After adding text:\n", list(fil))
```

Listing 7.4: Example7p4.py

As can be seen from the code, this is another way of opening the same file. But in this example, by using the **insert()** function, we can add characters into the text. Before inserting the text, we navigate to the beginning of the file by using the **seek()** function. Once the program runs, the following output will be obtained.

```
Before inserting the text:
 ['Hello!! This is\n', 'just a try for \n', 'a nice purpose.\n',
 'I like this text\n']
After adding text:
 ['Hello!! This is\n', 'Python is coming !!!just a try for \n',
 'a nice purpose.\n', 'I like this text\n']
```

◀

Example 7.5 Write a program that opens the same file saved after Example 7.4. The program should erase everything in the file. And then, it will write "This is a new text". Finally, the program will print the new content on the screen.

Solution. We just need to open the file in writing plus (w+) format(to overwrite and read it), and insert the new text into it. The following code can be used to accomplish the task.

```
#Example 7.5
#This example erases the content of the file and add a new text
MyText = "This is a new text"
```

```
f = open('Trying.txt','w+')
f.write("This is a new text")
f.seek(0)
Text = f.readlines()
print(Text)
```

Listing 7.5: Example7p5.py

Once the program runs, the following output will be obtained.

```
['This is a new text']
```

◀

7.2 PROBLEMS

7.1 Write a program that creates a file and writes "Hello my friend how are you doing?" in the first line. In the second line, it should write "This is just a shot". The file should be saved as "Try2.txt" into the directory.

7.2 Write a program that reads the file "Try2.txt" from the directory. The program will print the number of lines and the content on the screen.

7.3 Write a program that reads the same file as in Example 7.2. Then, it will add "This is strange" to the end of the text.

7.4 Write a program that reads the file created in Example 7.3. Then, add "Python is coming !!!" to the beginning of the file.

7.5 Write a program that opens the file saved after the previous example (Example 7.4). The program should erase everything in the file. And then, it will write "Python is a high level language" into it. Then, the program will print the new content on the screen.

Part II

SOFTWARE ENGINEERING TOOLS WITH PYTHON

Chapter 8

OBJECT-ORIENTED PROGRAMMING

The programming approach that we have so far applied to solve problems is called procedure-oriented programming (POP). We can manage to find a solution to any problem including the complex ones using POP. But when it comes to solve even more complex programming problems, it is recommended to use another approach which is called the object-oriented programming (OOP) technique. In the OOP technique, you can combine similar characteristics and put them all together to define objects. Once the objects are created, then, they can be used anywhere in the code as many times as necessary with more complex behaviors.

Programmers do not necessarily have to use OOP approach to write the codes. But to write more efficient and effective codes, we strongly recommend software engineers and programming professionals to learn the OOP approach.

Classes and objects are the most important concepts in OOP. An object is a special instantiation of a class. After a class is defined with methods (which are generally user-defined functions) and the variables in it, then, an object or multiple objects can be created referring to the same class.

8.1 Creating Classes

The word "class" is used to define a class. The syntax for defining a class can be shown as follows.

```
class  Nameofclass:
         body part
```

Example 8.1 Write a program that has a class named as "FirstClass". Then, a new variable named "Age" should be defined and a value of 25 should be assigned to it. And a method named "PrintHello" should be defined in that class, as well. Once the method "PrintHello" is called, it should print "Hello My Friend" on the screen.

Solution. The following code can be used to accomplish the task.

```
#Example 8.1
#This example shows a basic class with one variable and
# one method-which is a user defined function actually
class FirstClass:
    Age = 25
    def PrintHello(self):
        return print("Hello My Friend")
FirstObject = FirstClass()#Creating object with the class
FirstObject.PrintHello() #accessing an attribute
```

Listing 8.1: Example8p1.py

As it is seen above, in the **PrintHello** function that we defined, there is a phrase "**self**" between parentheses. This phrase comes in automatically as a first word once a function is created inside a class. By using the phrase "**self**", we will refer to the variables defined inside a function in later examples.

There is a **return** function at the last line of the PrintHello function. What it does is, once the function is called, it returns the value that comes immediately after it.

The object named "**FirstObject**" is created by assigning a class to it. Then, by using the object name as a first word followed by a dot, and then, writing the name of the method, or the name of the user-defined function inside the class, we can access the attribute.

Once the program runs, the following output will be obtained.

```
Hello My Friend
```

◀

Example 8.2 Write a program that has a class named "**Fight**". The class should have an attribute (variable) as five lives. It should have two methods, as well. The first method should calculate the left lives in case of an attack, and the second method should find out if the attacker is dead. You are required to create 2 objects as attackers from the class. Then, each attacker attacks twice, where the total number of attacks should be 5 and 4 for the first and the second attackers, respectively. Finally, the code should find out how many lives are left for each attacker.

Solution. The following code may be used to accomplish the task.

```
#Example 8.2
#This example shows how many life left for 2 fighters
class Fight:
    LeftLife = 5
    def Attack(self,number):
        print("We are under Attack!!!")
        self.LeftLife -= number
    def IsDead(self):
        if (self.LeftLife<=0):
            print("DEAD")
        else:
            print("I have " + str(self.LeftLife) + " life left over")

#Define objects
Fighter1 = Fight()
Fighter2 = Fight()

Fighter1.Attack(3)# Attack 3 times
Fighter1.Attack(2)# Attack 2 more times
Fighter1.IsDead()# Is Fighter1 dead ?

Fighter2.Attack(3)# Attack 3 times
Fighter2.Attack(1)# Attack 1 more time
Fighter2.IsDead()# Is Fighter2 dead ?
```

Listing 8.2: Example8p2.py

As it is seen above, 5 is assigned to the variable *LeftLife*. In order to use this variable inside the function *Attack*, or *IsDead*, we need to insert **self** and a **dot** before the variable LeftLife.

We can pass the number of lives inside the parentheses to the *Attack* function in the class after creating *Fighter1* and *Fighter2* objects. Once the program runs, the following output will be obtained.

```
We are under Attack!!!
We are under Attack!!!
DEAD
We are under Attack!!!
We are under Attack!!!
I have 1 life left over
```

◀

Example 8.3 Write a program that has a class named as "*Employees*" with "**__init__**" function. Two names with salaries will be sent to the class. And the information on names and salaries along with total number of employees will be printed on the screen.

Solution. What __init__ does is as soon as the class is called, it is initialized and run firstly as shown in the following code.

```
#Example 8.3
#This example shows a usage of the __init__ function in a class
class Employee:
    Counter = 0 # variable of Employee class
    def __init__(self, Name, Salary):
        self.name = Name
        self.salary = Salary
        Employee.Counter += 1

    def ShowEmployee(self):
        print("Name : {}  | Salary : {} | Total Employees : {}".
              format(self.name, self.salary, Employee.Counter))

#creating objects with initial values
Employ1 = Employee("Tiffany", 50000)
```

```
Employ2 = Employee("Eduardo", 70000)

Employ1.ShowEmployee()
Employ2.ShowEmployee()
```

Listing 8.3: Example8p3.py

As it can be seen above, the objects are created with the **__init__** function. For the variables inside the __init__ function, the prefix **self** is used. For the variable *Counter* which is outside the __init__ function, but inside the class, the name of the class *Employee* is used as prefix when it is used inside __init__. Once the program runs, the following output will be obtained.

```
Name : Tiffany  | Salary : 50000 | Total Employees : 2
Name : Eduardo  | Salary : 70000 | Total Employees : 2
```

◀

Example 8.4 Write a program that has a class named as "*Card*" which is about picking a card from a deck of 52 cards. Name of the user should be passed to the **__init__** function of the class. And the code should print the passed name and the picked card on the screen for three different players.

Solution. We need to use **random** module to select numbers randomly.

```
#Example 8.4
#This example picks card randomly
import random

class Card:
    # Define the suits
    SUITS = {1: 'Clubs', 2: 'Hearts', 3: 'Diamonds', 4: 'Spades'}
    # Define cards
    VALUES = {1: 'Ace',2: '2', 3: '3', 4: '4', 5: '5', 6: '6', 7: '7',
              8: '8', 9: '9', 10: '10', 11: 'Jack', 12: 'Queen', 13: 'King'}

    def __init__(self, name):
        self.Suit = random.randint(1,4)
        self.Value = random.randint(1,13)
        print("{}, you have {}- {} ".format(name, Card.SUITS[self.Suit],
```

```
                                            Card.VALUES[self.Value]))

card1 = Card("Henry")
card2 = Card("Jane")
card3 = Card("Floyd")
```

Listing 8.4: Example8p4.py

Once the code runs, the following output will be obtained.

```
Henry, you have Diamonds- 3
Jane, you have Diamonds- Jack
Floyd, you have Hearts- 2
```

◄

8.2 PROBLEMS

8.1 Write a program that has a class named "GUESS". A name should be passed to the class where the class should randomly select 6 numbers and print the name and the picked numbers on the screen.
8.2 Write a program that has a class named "Absolut". A float number should be passed to the class and the absolute value of the number should be printed on the screen.
8.3 Write a program that has a class named as "Employees" with the "**__init__**" function. Four names along with their corresponding ages will be sent to the class. And the information on names, ages and the total number of employees will be printed on the screen.
8.4 Write a program that has a class named "IsPrime". A number should be passed to the class, and the code should print YES or NO on the screen depending on whether the passed integer is positive or not.
8.5 Write a program that has a class named "Compare". Three numbers should be passed to the class. The code will put the entered numbers in order from the least to the greatest, and print them on the screen.

Chapter 9

WORKING WITH DATABASES

In this chapter, we will present how to work with **SQLite** databases. We will discuss how to create a database; add, delete, or change the data in a database, and query data in a database.

In order to read a created database, you need to install a database browser, or a database management tool. In this text, **DB Browser for SQLite** is used, which is an open source tool and can be downloaded from the web for different platforms.

To work with SQLite in Python, the **sqlite3** module should be imported to the program.

9.1 Creating A Database

By using the **connect()** function, a connection is created via sqlite3. There are some structures that must be written as they are, such as "**create table if not exists**", "**insert into**", or "**values**" which can be lower case or capital letters as shown in the following example.

Example 9.1 Write a program to create a database named "DataBTest.db" if it does not already exist.
Then, create the following table including the data in it.

Table 9.1: Sample table for Example 9.1

ID Number	First Name	Last Name	Address	Salary
1001	Iva	Casandra	101 Central St.	60000.21

Solution. The following code may be used to accomplish the given task.

```
#Example 9.1
#This example creates a database and inserts data in it.
import sqlite3
ConnectDB = sqlite3.connect("DataBTest.db") #connection object
# representing database
Cursor = ConnectDB.cursor()#get curser to execute sql statements

def CreateTable():
    Cursor.execute("CREATE TABLE IF NOT EXISTS SAMPLE (ID_NUMBER INT,"
                   "First_Name TEXT, Last_Name TEXT, Address TEXT,"
                   " Salary REAL)")
def AddToTable():
    Cursor.execute("INSERT INTO SAMPLE VALUES (1001,'Iva', 'Casandra', "
                   "'101 Central St.', 60000.21)")
    ConnectDB.commit() # save changes to database
    ConnectDB.close() # close database connection

CreateTable()
AddToTable()
```

Listing 9.1: Example9p1.py

◀

As can be seen above, the name of the created table is SAMPLE.

Once the program runs, the database will be created. If the database is opened, we will see the following under the Database Structure button.

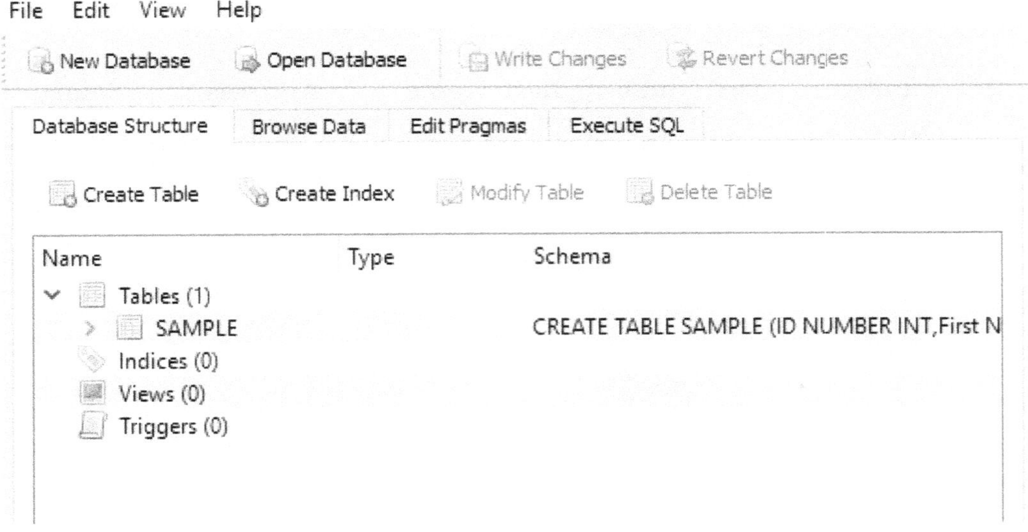

Figure 9.1: The table named SAMPLE which is created in Example 9.1

If you click on the Browse Data button, we will see that the data is inserted into the database.

Database Structure | Browse Data | Edit Pragmas | Execute SQL

Table: SAMPLE — New Record — Delete Record

	ID_NUMBER	First_Name	Last_Name	Address	Salary
	Filter	Filter	Filter	Filter	Filter
1	1001	Iva	Casandra	101 Central St.	60000.21

Figure 9.2: The Database created for the SAMPLE table

9.2 Adding More Data into Database

To add more data, **executemany()** function may be used and question marks (?) are placed for values as shown in the following example.

Example 9.2 Write a program that adds the following data into the SAMPLE table created in the previous example.

Table 9.2: Data to be added to the table, "SAMPLE"

ID Number	First Name	Last Name	Address	Salary
1001	Derek	Cruze	21 Central St.	30000
1002	Mike	Hand	502 Boulevard	45000.1
1102	Michelle	Castillo	121 Lake Side St.	52000.85
1057	Richard	Zennet	565 Leon Valley	100000.82
1065	Sylvia	Aguilar	2001 Martin St.	80000.91

Solution. The following code can be used to accomplish the task.

```
#Example 9.2
#This example adds more data in to a created database before
import sqlite3
ConnectDB = sqlite3.connect("DataBTest.db")
Cursor = ConnectDB.cursor()
MoreData = [(1001,'Derek', 'Cruze',"21 Central St.", 30000),
            (1002,'Mike', 'Hand',"502 Boulevard", 45000.1),
            (1102,'Michelle', 'Castillo',"121 Lake Side St.", 52000.85),
            (1057,'Richard', 'Zennet',"565 Leon Valley", 100000.82),
            (1065,'Sylvia', 'Aguilar',"2001 Martin St.", 80000.91)]
def AddToTable():
    Cursor.executemany("INSERT INTO SAMPLE VALUES (?,?,?,?,?)", MoreData)
    ConnectDB.commit() # save changes to database
    ConnectDB.close() # close database connection
```

```
AddToTable()
```

Listing 9.2: Example9p2.py

Once the program runs, the following output will be obtained in the database.

Database Structure | Browse Data | Edit Pragmas | Execute SQL

Table: SAMPLE | New Record | Delete Record

	ID_NUMBER	First_Name	Last_Name	Address	Salary
	Filter	Filter	Filter	Filter	Filter
1	1001	Iva	Casandra	101 Central St.	60000.21
2	1001	Derek	Cruze	21 Central St.	30000.0
3	1002	Mike	Hand	502 Boulevard	45000.1
4	1102	Michelle	Castillo	121 Lake Side...	52000.85
5	1057	Richard	Zennet	565 Leon Valley	100000.82
6	1065	Sylvia	Aguilar	2001 Martin St.	80000.91

Figure 9.3: Final outlook of database with added data

◀

9.3 Changing Data from A Database

By using some structural phrases such as "UPDATE", "SET", and "WHERE", data can be changed from a database as shown in the following example.

Example 9.3 Write a program that changes the salary of the person whose last name is "Hand" to 20000.

Solution. The following code can be used to accomplish the task.

```
#Example 9.3
#This example updates a data from database
import sqlite3
ConnectDB = sqlite3.connect("DataBTest.db")
Cursor = ConnectDB.cursor()

def Updating():
    Cursor.execute("UPDATE SAMPLE SET Salary = 20000 "
                   "WHERE Last_Name = 'Hand'")
    ConnectDB.commit()
    ConnectDB.close()

Updating()
```

Listing 9.3: Example9p3.py

Once the program runs, the following output will be obtained.

1	1001	Iva	Casandra	101 Central St.	60000.21
2	1001	Derek	Cruze	21 Central St.	30000.0
3	1002	Mike	Hand	502 Boulevard	20000.0
4	1102	Michelle	Castillo	121 Lake Side...	52000.85
5	1057	Richard	Zennet	565 Leon Valley	100000.82
6	1065	Sylvia	Aguilar	2001 Martin St.	80000.91

Figure 9.4: Final outlook of data after updating

◀

9.4 Deleting Data

Data can be deleted by using the phrases "DELETE FROM" and "WHERE" inside the **execute()** function as shown in the following example.

Example 9.4 Write a program that deletes the person whose first name is "Iva" from the database that was used in the previous example.

Solution. The following code can be used to accomplish the task.

```
#Example 9.4
#This example deletes data from a database
import sqlite3
ConnectDB = sqlite3.connect("DataBTest.db")
Cursor = ConnectDB.cursor()

def Deleting():
    Cursor.execute("DELETE FROM SAMPLE WHERE "
                   "First_Name = 'Iva'")
    ConnectDB.commit()
    ConnectDB.close()

Deleting()
```

Listing 9.4: Example9p4.py

Once the program runs, the following output will be obtained.

	ID_NUMBER	First_Name	Last_Name	Address	Salary
	Filter	Filter	Filter	Filter	Filter
1	1001	Derek	Cruze	21 Central St.	30000.0
2	1002	Mike	Hand	502 Boulevard	20000.0
3	1102	Michelle	Castillo	121 Lake Side...	52000.85
4	1057	Richard	Zennet	565 Leon Valley	100000.82
5	1065	Sylvia	Aguilar	2001 Martin St.	80000.91

Figure 9.5: Final outlook of the database after deleting data

As can be seen, the person whose first name is "Iva" does no longer appear in the list. ◀

9.5 Queries

By using "SELECT * FROM" and "WHERE" phrases as shown in the following example, we can search data within a database.

Example 9.5 Write a program that finds the person whose first name is "Derek" to print all the data belonging to that person on the screen. Then, the code should print every person's data on the screen, as well.

Solution. The following code can be used to accomplish the task.

```
#Example 9.5
#This example queries data
import sqlite3
ConnectDB = sqlite3.connect("DataBTest.db")
Cursor = ConnectDB.cursor()

def Searching():
    Cursor.execute("SELECT * FROM SAMPLE WHERE"
                   " First_Name = 'Derek'")
    print("Searching a sigle data")
    print(Cursor.fetchall())

def ShowAll():
    for EachRow in Cursor.execute("SELECT * FROM "
                    "SAMPLE ORDER BY First_Name"):
        print(EachRow)
    ConnectDB.close()

Searching()
print("Printing the whole data")
ShowAll()
```

Listing 9.5: Example9p5.py

Once the program runs, the following output will be obtained.

```
Searching a sigle data
[(1001, 'Derek', 'Cruze', '21 Central St.', 30000.0)]
Printing the whole data
```

```
(1001, 'Derek', 'Cruze', '21 Central St.', 30000.0)
(1102, 'Michelle', 'Castillo', '121 Lake Side St.', 52000.85)
(1002, 'Mike', 'Hand', '502 Boulevard', 20000.0)
(1057, 'Richard', 'Zennet', '565 Leon Valley', 100000.82)
(1065, 'Sylvia', 'Aguilar', '2001 Martin St.', 80000.91)
```

◀

9.6 PROBLEMS

9.1 Write a program that creates a database called "TestDataB.db" if it does not already exist. Then, create the table below including the data in it. Name of the table should be "TESTING".

Table 9.3: TESTING table

Number	**FName**	**LName**	**Salary**
15	Melo	Dona	10000

9.2 Write a program that adds the following data into the table called TESTING, which was created in the previous example.

Table 9.4: Data to be added to the table

Number	**FName**	**LName**	**Salary**
45	Brown	Johnson	45000
85	Brown	Casanova	90000

9.3 Referring to the table in the previous example, write a program that changes the salary of the person who makes 45000 to 20000.

9.4 Write a program that deletes the person whose data for "FName" is "Brown" from the database obtained in Example 9.2. The code should print the final version of the list on the screen.

9.5 Referring to the table obtained in Example 9.2, write a program that finds the person whose data for "Lname" is "Dona", and prints all the data belonging to that person on the screen.

Part III

SELECTED TOPICS IN PYTHON

Chapter 10

MATRIX ALGEBRA

In this chapter, we will present how to perform matrix calculations in Python by using the Numpy module. Numpy stands for NUMerical PYthon. This module has many features that makes Python a very powerful tool to perform numerical and scientific computing together with the Scipy (SCIentific PYthon) module.

In numpy, a new data structure will be encountered, which is called an **array**. Arrays are indexed lists. An easy way to produce arrays is to use the **linspace()** or **arange()** functions in numpy.

10.1 Using linspace and arange Functions

Data type for the numbers produced via the linspace() and arange() functions is numpy.ndarray. It can be interpreted as "N Dimensional array in **numpy** module".

We have already learned lists as a data type earlier in this book. We can think of ndarrays as multi-dimensional containers of items. However, since we will work only with the numbers in this chapter, ndarrays can be regarded as multi-dimensional matrices.

To illustrate the ndarrays data type, we shall now create 4 **equally spaced numbers** from 0 to 12 by using the linspace() function at Python console as follows.

```
>>> import numpy as np
>>> XValues = np.linspace(0,12,4)
>>> XValues
```

```
array([ 0.,   4.,   8.,  12.])
>>> print(type(XValues))
<class 'numpy.ndarray'>
>>>
```

In addition, the arange() function can be used for similar purposes. As an example, we may type the following at the Python console to create numbers from 2 to 10.

```
>>> import numpy as np
>>> x = np.arange(2,11)
>>> x
array([ 2,  3,  4,  5,  6,  7,  8,  9, 10])
>>> print(type(x))
<class 'numpy.ndarray'>
>>>
```

As it is seen, number 11 is excluded from the produced numbers.

The arange() function can be used to produce a sequence of numbers where the difference between numbers can be specified as well.

```
>>> import numpy as np
>>> x = np.arange(2,5,0.2)
>>> x
array([ 2. ,  2.2,  2.4,  2.6,  2.8,  3. ,  3.2,  3.4,  3.6,  3.8,  4. ,
        4.2,  4.4,  4.6,  4.8])
>>>
```

Above,the command arange(2,5,0.2) creates numbers between 2(included) and 5(excluded) with the increment of 0.2.

10.2 Creating Multidimensional Arrays

Inside the **numpy** module, **array** and **matrix** classes are available to create multi-dimensional arrays. The array class is used to create n dimensional arrays for general purposes in scientific applications, while the **matrix** class is used for calculations performed in Linear Algebra.

Example 10.1 Write a code to create a 2 dimensional 4 by 3 array by using array() function.Produce the same array by using the matrix() function, as well. Then, the code should print the elements at $(2,3)$, along with the sizes of the arrays and data types for both arrays on the screen.

Solution. The following code may be used to accomplish the tasks.

```
#Example 10.1
#This example creates 2-dimensional data by
# using array and matrix functions
import numpy as np
x = np.array([[1,2,3],[4,5,6],[7,8,9],[10,11,12]])
y = np.matrix("[1,2,3;4,5,6;7,8,9;10,11,12]")
print("Values for x : \n", x)
print("Value of x(2,3) is : ", x[1][2])#indexing starts from 0
print("Shape/Size of x : ", x.shape)
print("Data type of x : ", type(x))
print("Values for y : \n", y)
print("Value of y(2,3) is : ", y[1,2])
print("Shape/Size of y : ", y.shape)
print("Data type of y : ", type(y))
```

Listing 10.1: Example10p1.py

In the code, the numbers for the elements of the array are selected from 1 to 12. Once the code runs, we obtain the following result.

```
Values for x :
 [[ 1  2  3]
 [ 4  5  6]
 [ 7  8  9]
 [10 11 12]]
Value of x(2,3) is :  6
Shape/Size of x :  (4, 3)
Data type of x :  <class 'numpy.ndarray'>
Values for y :
```

```
 [[ 1  2  3]
 [ 4  5  6]
 [ 7  8  9]
 [10 11 12]]
Value of y(2,3) is :  6
Shape/Size of y :  (4, 3)
Data type of y :  <class 'numpy.matrixlib.defmatrix.matrix'>
```

◄

Example 10.2 Write a code to create two 3 dimensional 2 by 4 arrays. The first array should have numbers from 1 to 24, assigned to the variable x, and the second array should have zeros for all elements, assigned to the variable *init*. The code should print two elements of x on the screen. The first element to be printed is at the 2nd row of the 3rd column from the 2nd dimension (x(2,2,3)). The second element is at the 1st row of the 4th column from the 3rd dimension (x(3,1,4)). Then the shape of x should be printed on the screen as well. Next, the code should assign the 1st row of x from 2nd dimension to the location of 2nd row of the 1st dimension in *init* (x(2,1,all elements) → init(1,2,all elements)). Finally, the code should print the elements of *init* on the screen.

Solution. The following code may be used to accomplish the tasks.

```
#Example 10.2
#This example initializes and creates 3-dimensional array
import numpy as np
init = np.zeros((3,2,4))
x = np.array([[[1,2,3,4],[5,6,7,8]],
              [[9,10,11,12],[13,14,15,16]],
              [[17,18,19,20],[21,22,23,24]]])
print("Values for x : \n", x)
print("Value of x(2,2,3) is : ", x[1][1][2])
print("Value of x(3,1,4) is : ", x[2,0,3])
print("Shape/Size of x : ", x.shape)
print("****************************")
init[0,1,:] = x[1,0,:]
print("Values for init :\n", init)
```

Listing 10.2: Example10p2.py

An array can be initialized by using the **zeros()** function within the numpy module, where zeros are assigned to all elements as written in the code.

Once the code runs, we obtain the following result.

```
Values for x :
 [[[ 1  2  3  4]
  [ 5  6  7  8]]

 [[ 9 10 11 12]
  [13 14 15 16]]

 [[17 18 19 20]
  [21 22 23 24]]]
Value of x(2,2,3) is :  15
Value of x(3,1,4) is :  20
Shape/Size of x :  (3, 2, 4)
******************************
Values for init :
 [[[  0.   0.   0.   0.]
  [  9.  10.  11.  12.]]

 [[  0.   0.   0.   0.]
  [  0.   0.   0.   0.]]

 [[  0.   0.   0.   0.]
  [  0.   0.   0.   0.]]]
```

◀

10.3 Special Matrices

There are very useful functions available to create special types of matrices. They make life easier for the programmer. Ideally, these functions are called **methods**. However, we will treat them as built-in functions within the modules just mentioned. Therefore, here and for the rest of the book, we will call such commands as **functions** in order to make the **terminology** familiar to the programmers having no or little knowledge about object-oriented programming and classes.

Table 10.1: Some of the available special matrices in **numpy** module

Function	**Description**
zeros((a,b))	creates an array with zeros of the size a by b
ones((a,b))	creates an array with ones of the size a by b
eye(a)	creates an identity square matrix of the size a by a
diag([a,b,c])	creates a matrix whose diagonal elements are a, b, and c
empty((a,b))	creates an a by b empty array

Example 10.3 Write a code to create two matrices. The first matrix should be created by using the **eye()** function, where the diagonal elements are $[30, 30, 30]$. The second matrix should be created by using the **diag()** function where the diagonal elements are $[25, 15, 5]$. The code should print the sum of these matrices on the screen.

Solution. The following code may be used to accomplish the given tasks.

```
#Example 10.3
#This example uses eye and diag functions
import numpy as np
X = np.eye(3)*10
Diag = np.diag([25,15,5])
print(Diag + X)
```

Listing 10.3: Example10p3.py

Once the code runs, the following result will be obtained.

```
[[ 35.   0.   0.]
 [  0.  25.   0.]
 [  0.   0.  15.]]
```

◄

10.4 Operations on Matrices

We can add or subtract matrices in a simple way as shown in the previous example. For multiplication, the result depends on whether the matrices are created by using the array() or the matrix() functions. Matrices created by the matrix() function are 2-dimensional, while matrices created by the array() function can be of any dimension in the numpy module. If A and B are created using the matrix() function, then A*B gives the matrix multiplication of A and B. However, if A and B are created using the array() function, then A*B gives the result of the element-wise multiplication. To perform a regular multiplication of A and B matrices, we need to use the **dot()** function as numpy.dot(A,B).

Please note that in order to multiply the matrices, the number of columns of the first matrix (matrix A in this case) should be equal to the number of rows of the second matrix (matrix B in this case).

For element-wise dividing, A / B is used no matter how the matrices are created (by using the array() function or the matrix() function).

Example 10.4 Write a code that has two matrices as $[1,2,3;4,5,6;7,8,9]$ and $[1,0,0;0,5,0;0,0,10]$. The matrices should be created by using both matrix() and array() functions. Then, the code should print the products of these matrices with the multiplication operator (*) and the dot() function.

Solution. The following code can be used to accomplish the tasks.

```
#Example 10.4
#This example shows multiplications of
# matrices created by matrix() and array() functions
import numpy as np
X = np.matrix("[1, 2, 3;4, 5, 6;7, 8, 9]")
Y = np.matrix("[1, 0, 0;0, 5, 0;0, 0, 10]")
XX = np.array([[1,2,3],[4,5,6],[7,8,9]])
YY = np.array([[1,0,0],[0,5,0],[0,0,10]])
print("Multiplying X and Y created with matrix():\n", X*Y)
print("Multiplying XX and YY created with array():\n", XX*YY)
```

```
print("Multiplying X and Y with dot():\n", np.dot(X,Y))
print("Multiplying XX and YY with dot():\n",np.dot(XX,YY))
```

Listing 10.4: Example10p4.py

Once the code runs, the following result will be obtained.

```
Multiplying X and Y created with matrix():
 [[ 1 10 30]
 [ 4 25 60]
 [ 7 40 90]]
Multiplying XX and YY created with array():
 [[ 1  0  0]
 [ 0 25  0]
 [ 0  0 90]]
Multiplying X and Y with dot():
 [[ 1 10 30]
 [ 4 25 60]
 [ 7 40 90]]
Multiplying XX and YY with dot():
 [[ 1 10 30]
 [ 4 25 60]
 [ 7 40 90]]
```

◄

Some useful functions in the numpy module are available to perform algebraic calculations on matrices.

Table 10.2: Some of the available calculation tools in Python

Function	**Description**
a.conj().transpose()	calculates the transpose of matrix a
numpy.linalg.det(a)	calculates the determinant of matrix a
numpy.linalg.inv(a)	calculates the inverse of matrix a
numpy.rank(a)	calculates the rank of matrix a
numpy.linalg.norm(a, ord=Y)	calculates the norm of matrix a for order Y

Example 10.5 Write a code to calculate the transpose and ∞, 1, and 2 norms of the matrix given by $[1, 2, 3; 4, 5, 6; 7, 8, 9]$.

Solution. The following code can be used to accomplish the tasks.

```
#Example 10.5
#This example calculates transpose and norms
import numpy as np
from numpy import linalg as lina
X = np.array([[1,2,3],[4,5,6],[7,8,9]])
Trn = X.conj().transpose()
print("Transpose of X is :\n", Trn)
print("inf-Norm :\n", lina.norm(X, ord=np.inf))
print("1-Norm :\n", lina.norm(X, ord=1))
print("2-Norm :\n", lina.norm(X, ord=2))
```

Listing 10.5: Example10p5.py

Once the code runs, we will obtain the following result.

```
Transpose of X is :
 [[1 4 7]
 [2 5 8]
 [3 6 9]]
inf-Norm :
 24.0
```

```
1-Norm :
 18.0
2-Norm :
 16.8481033526
```

◀

10.4.1 Dot Product

Dot product, sometimes called the inner product, is the sum of all products of the two vectors where multiplication is performed element-wise. Let A and B be vectors having length n as below.

$$A_i = [A_1, A_2, A_3, ..., A_n], i = 1, 2, 3, .., n$$

$$B_i = [B_1, B_2, B_3, ..., B_n], i = 1, 2, 3, .., n$$

Their dot product can be mathematically represented as

$$A * B = \sum_{i=1}^{n} A_i * B_i$$

$$= A_1B_1 + A_2B_2 + A_3B_3 + ... + A_nB_n$$

Since the result is a scalar number, it is also called a scalar product.

The function that calculates the dot product of two vectors, A and B, is **dot(A,B)** in the numpy module.

Remark 1. The inner product of two vectors, u and v, is defined by $u * v = |\mathrm{u}||\mathrm{v}|cos\theta$ where |u| and |v| are the norms of the vectors u and v respectively. θ is the angle between vectors u and v.

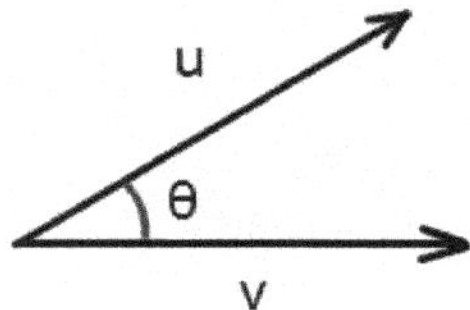

Figure 10.1: Angle between two vectors

Example 10.6 Write a code that calculates the angle between the vectors $u = 2i - j + k$ and $v = i + j + 3k$ by using the dot product.

Solution. The following code can be used to accomplish the tasks.

```
#Example 10.6
#This example calculates dot product
#  and angle between two vectors
import numpy as np
from numpy import linalg as lina
u=[2,-1,1]
v=[1,1,3]
x = np.array(u)
y = np.array(v)
Dot = np.dot(x,y)
print("Value of Dot product is :", Dot)
CosAngle = Dot/((lina.norm(x)*lina.norm(y)))
print("Angle in terms of Radian is :", CosAngle)
Theta = np.arccos(CosAngle)*(180/np.pi)
print("Angle in terms of Degree is :", Theta)
```

Listing 10.6: Example10p6.py

Once the code runs, we will obtain the following result.

```
Value of Dot product is : 4
Angle in terms of Radian is : 0.492365963917
Angle in terms of Degree is : 60.5037915034
```

◀

10.4.2 Cross Product

Cross product is also known as the **vector product**. If A and B are two vectors, then, the cross product of A and B should be defined in three-dimensional space, R^3. Let $A = [A_1, A_2, A_3]$ and $B = [B_1, B_2, B_3]$. Then the cross product of A and B is defined as

$$AxB = \left[\begin{vmatrix} A_2 & A_3 \\ B_2 & B_3 \end{vmatrix}, \begin{vmatrix} A_1 & A_3 \\ B_1 & B_3 \end{vmatrix}, \begin{vmatrix} A_1 & A_2 \\ B_1 & B_2 \end{vmatrix} \right]$$

$$= [A_2B_3 - A_3B_2, A_3B_1 - A_1B_3, A_1B_2 - A_2B_1]$$

The resulting vector is perpendicular to the vectors being multiplied. The cross product is defined by the following Remark:

Remark 2. The cross product of two vectors, A and B, is defined by A x B = |A||B|$sin\theta$ n where |A| and |B| are the magnitudes of the vectors A and B respectively and n is a unit vector. θ is the angle between vectors A and B.

The function that is used to calculate the cross product of two vectors, A and B, is **cross(A,B)** in numpy.

Example 10.7 Write a code that calculates the angle between vectors $u = 2i – j + k$ and $v = i + j + 3k$ by using the cross product.

Solution. The following code can be used to accomplish the given task.

```
#Example 10.7
#This example calculates cross product
#  and angle between two vectors
import numpy as np
from numpy import linalg as lina
u=[2,-1,1]
v=[1,1,3]
x = np.array(u)
y = np.array(v)
Cros = np.cross(x,y)
print("Result of Cross product is :", Cros)
SinAngle = lina.norm(Cros)/((lina.norm(x)*lina.norm(y)))
print("Angle in terms of Radian is :", SinAngle)
Theta = np.arcsin(SinAngle)*(180/np.pi)
print("Angle in terms of Degree is :", Theta)
```

Listing 10.7: Example10p7.py

Once the code runs, we will obtain the following result.

```
Result of Cross product is : [-4 -5  3]
Angle in terms of Radian is : 0.870388279778
Angle in terms of Degree is : 60.5037915034
```

◀

10.5 System of Linear Equations

Systems of linear equations can be represented as in the form of $Ax = B$ where A is a square matrix and B is a column vector. To solve this system, **solve()** function in **linalg** sub-package can be used within the numpy module (**numpy.linalg.solve()**).

Example 10.8 Write a code to solve the following system.

$$\begin{cases} 2x + y - z = 1 \\ x + y - z = 0 \\ 6x - 3y + z = 3 \end{cases}$$

Solution. The following code can be used to accomplish the given task.

```
#Example 10.8
#This example solves a system of linear equations
import numpy as np
from numpy import linalg as LA
A = np.array([[2, 1, -1],[1, 1, -1],[6, -3, 1]])
B = np.array([[1],[0],[3]])
Result = LA.solve(A,B)
print("x, y, z :\n", Result)
```

Listing 10.8: Example10p8.py

Once the code runs, we will obtain the following result.

```
x, y, z :
 [[ 1.]
 [ 2.]
 [ 3.]]
```

◀

10.6 PROBLEMS

10.1 Write a code that creates a 2 dimensional 2 by 3 array by using the array() function where the elements are picked randomly. Then, the code should print the element at $(2, 2)$ on the screen.

10.2 Write a code to create two matrices. The first matrix should be created by using the eye() function where the diagonal elements are $[50, 50]$. The second matrix should be created using the diag() function where the diagonal elements are $[20, 10]$. The code should print the sum of these matrices on the screen.

10.3 Write a code to create two 3 by 3 matrices. The elements should be integers picked randomly between 1 and 100. Then, the code should print the element-wise multiplication of these matrices on the screen.

10.4 Write a code that calculates the angle between the vectors $u = i + 2j + 4k$ and $v = -7i + 8j + 10k$ using the dot product.

10.5 Write a code that calculates the angle between the vectors $u = i + 2j + 4k$ and $v = -7i + 8j + 10k$ using the cross product.

10.6 Write a code to solve the following system.

$$\begin{cases} x + 2y + 3z = 10 \\ 2x - y - z = 5 \\ 4x + 2y + 8z = 0 \end{cases}$$

Chapter 11

PLOTTING GRAPHICS

, In this chapter, we will discuss how to plot two-dimensional graphics in Python. We will use the **pyplot()** function within the **matplotlib** module and **numpy** module.

Matplotlib and Numpy modules have very useful functions that make Python a very powerful tool for plotting the results of numerical calculations. In this regard, these modules have similar features with MATLAB[1].

Generally, list data types, and multidimensional arrays, known as ndarrays from numpy module, are used to represent values for plotting.

11.1 Single Plots

Single plots are produced by using the **plot()** function from **matplotlib.pyplot**. To show the plotted image, **show()** function must be used. When we use show(), we must be careful where to insert this function. If it is placed before the labeling, the labels may not be shown. Therefore, it is recommended to place it on the last lines of code when showing figures depending on the case.

Example 11.1 Write a code that creates 4 equally spaced x values from 0 to 12. Corresponding y values are given as $y = [2, 3, 8, 20]$. The program should plot the x values and the corresponding y values.

[1]MATLAB is a registered trademark of The MathWorks, Inc.

Solution. The following code may be used to accomplish the task.

```
#Example 11.1
#This example plots x values corresponding to y values
import matplotlib.pyplot as plt
import numpy as np
XValues = np.linspace(0,12,4)
#linspace() creates 4 values above from 0 to 12 equally spaced
YValues = [2, 3, 8, 20]
plt.plot(XValues, YValues)
plt.ylabel('y values')
plt.xlabel('x values')
plt.title('This is title')
plt.legend(["Values"])
plt.show() # put this line after labels
```

Listing 11.1: Example11p1.py

In the code above, **linspace()** function creates 4 equally spaced numbers from 0 to 12. The following figure presents the output of the code.

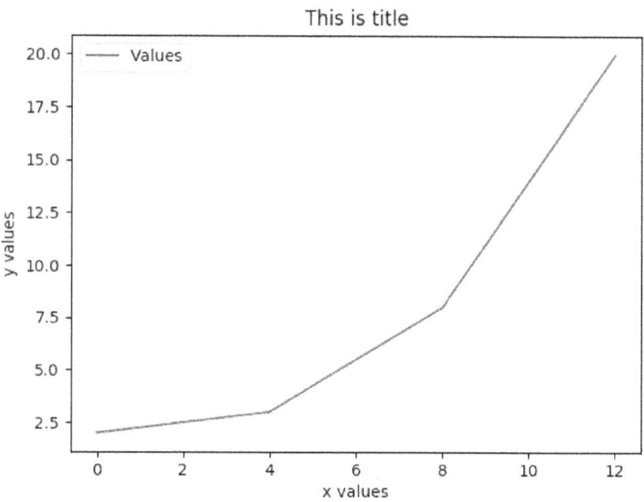

Figure 11.1: Output of Example 11.1

◀

On the left hand side of the upper corner of the figure, , "Values" is placed via the **legend()** function.

Example 11.2 Write a program that plots the graph of the numbers in the list $L = [1, 2, 3, 4]$.

Solution. The following code may be used to accomplish the task.

```
#Example 11.2
#This example plots just a list of values
import matplotlib.pyplot as plt
MyList = [1,2,3,4]
plt.plot(MyList)
plt.ylabel('y values')
plt.xlabel('x values')
plt.title('This is title')
plt.legend(["Values"])
plt.grid(True)
plt.show()
```

Listing 11.2: Example11p2.py

The following figure is the output of the run code.

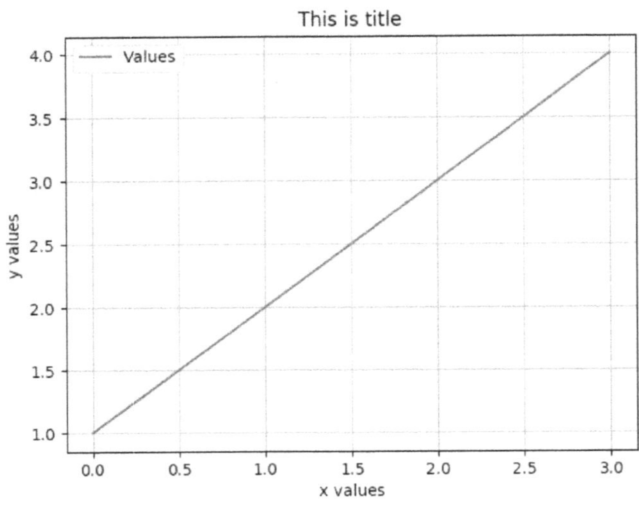

Figure 11.2: Output of Example 11.2

◀

As shown in the figure, the values of the list L lie on the coordinate axis. And since no value corresponds to the x values and range values start with 0 in Python, these values are automatically generated as $[0, 1, 2, 3]$. In the code, the **grid (True)** function puts the grids on.

Example 11.3 Write a program that plots the graph of y, where $0 \leq x \leq 2\pi$, y=cos(x).

Solution. The following code can be used to accomplish the given task.

```
#Example 11.3
#This example plots cosine of an array
import matplotlib.pyplot as plt
from math import pi as pi
import numpy as np
x = np.linspace(0,2*pi, 100) #creates 100 numbers
y = np.cos(x) # do not be confused with math.cos(x)
plt.plot(x, y, 'c—') #different styles are possible
plt.axis([0, 2*pi, -2, 2]) # [xmin, xmax, ymin, ymax]
plt.ylabel('y values')
plt.xlabel('x values')
plt.title('This is title')
plt.legend(["Values"])
plt.grid(True)
plt.show()
```

Listing 11.3: Example11p3.py

The interval is divided into 100 points via the code. Therefore, the number of elements of x is 100. To calculate the y values, when y = math.cos(x) is used, an error occurs which reads "x is not a scalar". Thus, in such cases the function, i.e. cosine in this case, should be calculated using the numpy module as in the given code. In this code, the **plot()** function is used with 'c–' style. Here 'c' represents the cyan color, and '–' represents the dashed line style. There exists a remarkable number of styles for colors and lines available in Python.

Once the code runs, we will obtain the following figure as the output.

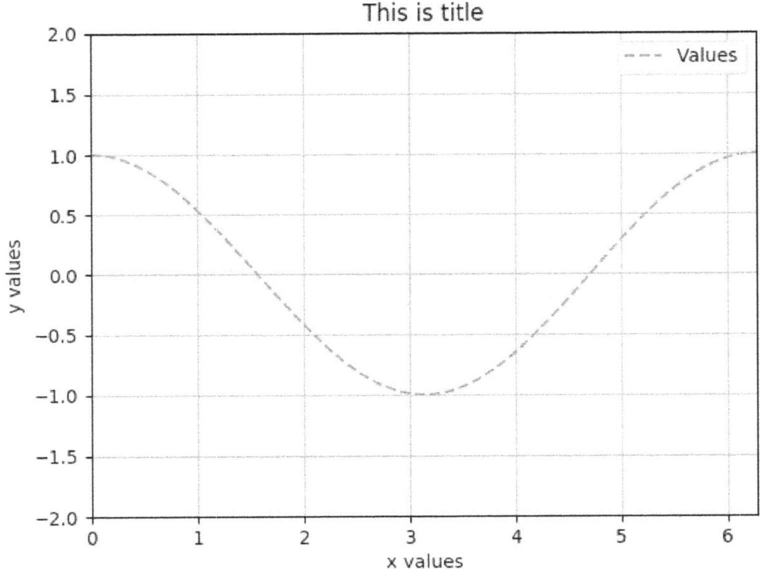

Figure 11.3: Output of Example 11.3

◀

Table 11.1: Some of available colors with **plot()** function

Character	**Corresponding Color**
"b"	blue color
"g"	green color
"r"	red color
"m"	magenta color
"c"	cyan color
"k"	black color

Table 11.2: Some of the available line styles for the **plot()** function

Character	**Description for style of line**
”-”	Solid line style
”–”	Dashed line style
”.”	Point marker for line
”*”	Star marker as line

11.2 Multiple Plots

More than one graph can be plotted on a single figure. This is achieved in 2 different ways. We may have multiple plots on the same coordinate system, or separate coordinates in one figure.

11.2.1 Plots on A Single Coordinate System

By using multiple parameters in the plot() function as shown in the following example, more than one plot can be made possible.

Example 11.4 Write a program that plots the variables y1, y2 and y3 where y1 = sin(x), y2 = cos(x), y3 = y1 + y2 for $0 \leq x \leq 2\pi$, on a single coordinate system.

Solution. The following code may be used to accomplish the task.

```
#Example 11.4
#This example plots 3 graphs on a single coordinate
import numpy as np
from math import pi as pi
import matplotlib.pyplot as plt
x = np.linspace(0,2*pi, 80) #creates 80 numbers
y1 = np.sin(x)
y2 = np.cos(x)
y3 = y1 + y2
plt.plot(x, y1, 'r-.', x, y2, 'k+', x, y3, 'gh')
```

```
plt.ylabel('y values')
plt.xlabel('x values')
plt.title('Graph of y1, y2 and y3')
plt.legend(["y1=sin(x)", "y2=cos(x)", "y3=y1+y2"])
plt.grid(True)
plt.show()
```

Listing 11.4: Example11p4.py

In order to plot multiple graphs, we pair domain and range values together with the optional line and color styles inside the plot() function.

Once the code is run, we get the following figure as output.

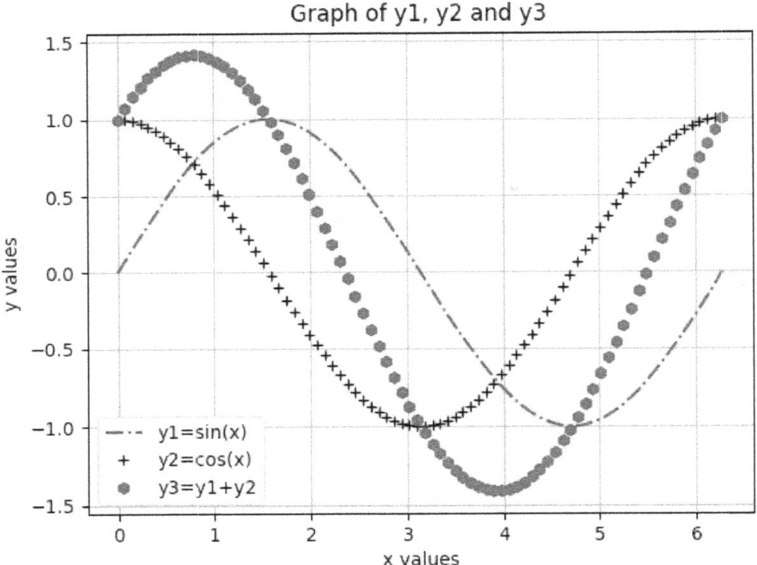

Figure 11.4: Output of Example 11.4

◀

11.2.2 Multiple Plots with Multiple Axes on A Figure

Multiple plots can be drawn by using the **subplot()** and **plot()** functions.

Example 11.5 Write a program that plots the variables y1, y2, y3 and y4 where y1 = sin(x), y2 = cos(x), y3 = y1 + y2, y4 = y1-y2 for $0 \leq x \leq 2\pi$, with 4 different axes on a figure.

Solution. The following code may be used to accomplish the task.

```
#Example 11.5
#This example plots 4 graphs on 4 axes on 1 figure
import numpy as np
import matplotlib.pyplot as plt
from math import pi as pi
x = np.linspace(0,2*pi, 80) #creates 80 numbers
y1 = np.sin(x)
y2 = np.cos(x)
y3 = y1 + y2
y4 = y1 - y2
plt.figure(1)
plt.subplot(221)
plt.plot(x,y1)
plt.title('1st Graph')
plt.subplot(222)
plt.plot(x,y2)
plt.title('2nd Graph')
plt.subplot(223)
plt.plot(x,y3)
plt.title('3rd Graph')
plt.subplot(224)
plt.plot(x,y4)
plt.title('4th Graph')
plt.show()
```

Listing 11.5: Example11p5.py

Above, in the subplot() function, there are three numbers between the parentheses. The first number sets the number of rows of the figure, the second number specifies the total number of columns of the figure and the last number specifies the location of the plot within the figure.

Once the code runs, we obtain the following as the output.

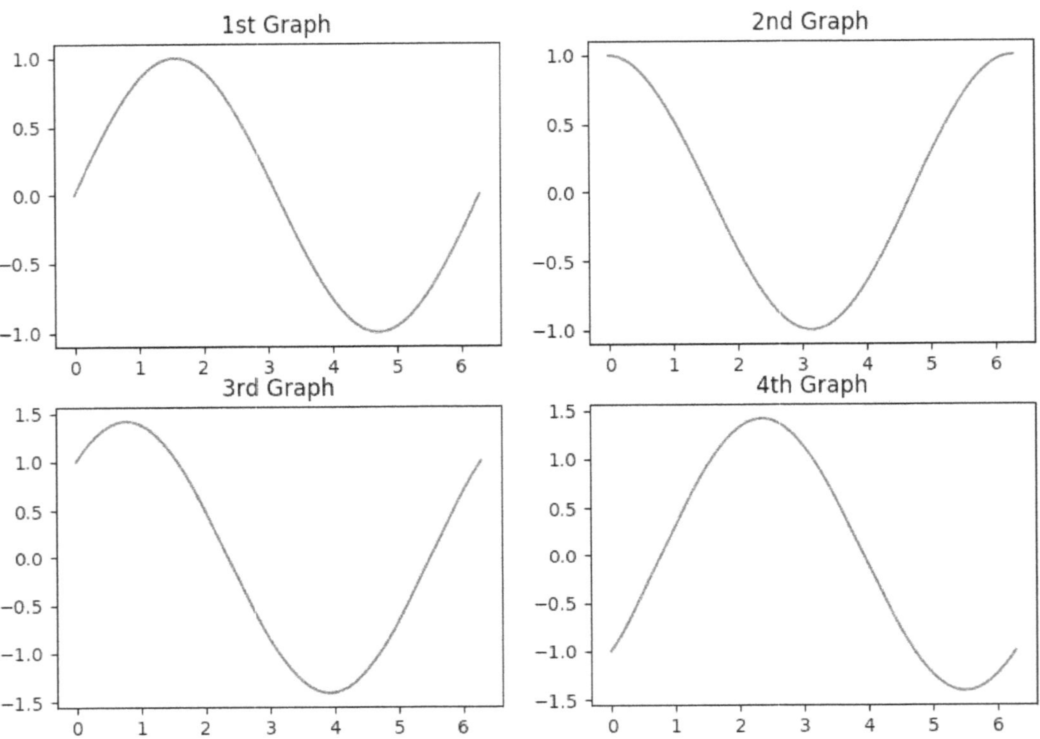

Figure 11.5: Output of Example 11.5

◀

11.3 Plotting with Different Functions

There are different functions to plot different type of graphics in Python , some of which are listed in Table 11.3.

Table 11.3: Some of available plotting functions in Python

Function	Description
bar	It plots a bar graph
contour	It plots contours
hist	It plots a histogram
loglog	It makes a plot with log scaling
pie	It plots a pie chart
polar	It makes a polar plot

Example 11.6 Write a program that plots a pie graph for the data given as; Cars-35%, Trucks-20%, TIR-15% Planes-30%.

Solution. The following code can be used to accomplish the task.

```
#Example 11.6
#This example plots a pie chart
import matplotlib.pyplot as plt
Labels = "Cars", "Trucks", "TIR", "Planes"
Percentages = [35, 20, 15, 30]
Figure1, Axis1 = plt.subplots()
Axis1.pie(Percentages, labels = Labels)
plt.title('Pie Graph of DATA')
plt.show()
```

Listing 11.6: Example11p6.py

Once the code runs, we obtain the following as the output.

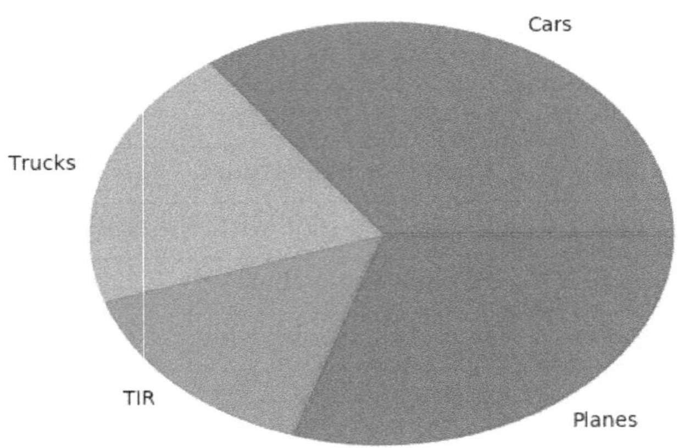

Figure 11.6: Output of Example 11.6

◀

11.4 PROBLEMS

11.1 Write a code that creates 20 equally spaced x values from 0 to 40. Corresponding y values should be chosen randomly from integers between 1 and 100. The program should plot x values and corresponding y values.

11.2 Write a program that plots the graph of the numbers in the list $L = [5, 6, 7, 8, 12, 15]$. Explain the reason of assigning x values in the graph.

11.3 Write a program that plots the graph of y=tan(x), where $0 \leq x \leq \pi$.

11.4 Write a program that plots both y1 and y2 where y1 = sin(5x), y2 = cos(4x), for $0 \leq x \leq 2\pi$, on a single coordinate system.

11.5 Write a program that plots y1, y2, y3 and y4 where y1 = sin(2x), y2 = sin(3x), y3 = sin(4x), y4 = sin(5x) for $0 \leq x \leq \pi$; with an individual axis for each variable on a figure.

11.6 Write a program that plots a pie graph for the following data: Human-55%, Animals-40%, and Zombie-5%.

Chapter 12

SYMBOLIC CALCULATIONS

In this chapter, we will first present how to compute mathematical operations symbolically. Then, evaluation of the expressions and equations at a special point will be examined.

The **sympy** module is used to perform symbolic calculations in Python. There are various calculations that can be carried out using this module. Before the calculations, related variables should be defined as symbols to the interpreter.

12.1 Symbolic Mathematics

By using the sympy module, operations including solving algebraic equations; finding limits, derivatives, and integrals of functions; solving ordinary and partial differential equations can be carried out.

12.1.1 Solving Algebraic Equations

There exist very useful functions in sympy for performing symbolic algebraic operations.

Table 12.1: Some of the algebraic functions available in sympy

Function	Description
apart	applies partial fraction decomposition on rational functions
cancel	writes rational functions with no common factors
collect	collects like terms
expand	writes the expressions in an expanded form
factor	factors entered polynomials
simplify	simplifies the expression
solve	solves algebraic equations
solve_linear_system	solves a system of linear equations

Example 12.1 Rewrite the following algebraic equation in its simplest form using the **cancel()** function.

$$y = \frac{(x+2)(x-1)}{x^2-4}$$

Solution. The following code can be used to accomplish the task.

```
#Example 12.1
#This example cancels the like terms in a fraction
from sympy import *
x = symbols('x')
y = ((x + 2)*(x - 1))/(x**2-4)
Result = cancel(y)
print(Result)
```

Listing 12.1: Example12p1.py

Once the code runs, we will get the following result.

```
(x - 1)/(x - 2)
```

◀

Example 12.2 Write a code to solve the equation, $y = 2x^3 - 8x^2 + 2x + 12$.

Solution. The following code can be used to solve the equation.

```
#Example 12.2
#This example solves an equation
from sympy import *
x = Symbol('x')
y = solve(2*x**3-8*x**2 + 2*x + 12)
print(y)
```

Listing 12.2: Example12p2.py

Once the code runs, we will obtain the following result.

```
[-1, 2, 3]
```

◀

Example 12.3 Write a code to solve the systems of equations.

$$System1: \begin{cases} x + 2y - z = 2 \\ 3x - 6y + 5z = 6 \\ 4x + 3y + z = 13 \end{cases}$$

$$System2: \begin{cases} 2x + y = 20 \\ -5x + 2y = -5 \end{cases}$$

Solution. The following code may be used to accomplish the task.

```
#Example 12.3
#This example solves two systems of linear equations
from sympy import Matrix, solve_linear_system
from sympy.abc import x, y, z
System1 = Matrix(((1, 2, -1, 2), (3, -6, 5, 6), (4, 3, 1, 13)))
System2 = Matrix(((2, 1, 20), (-5, 2, -5)))
Result1 = solve_linear_system(System1, x, y, z)
Result2 = solve_linear_system(System2, x, y)
print("The result of 1st system is : ",Result1)
print("The result of 2nd system is : ",Result2)
```

Listing 12.3: Example12p3.py

To identify equations in Python, the variables should be on one side, and the constant terms should be on the other side of the equation. Then, all coefficients should be written inside the matrix as seen in the code. Finally, the system of equations can be solved using the **solve_linear_system()** function.

Once the code runs, we will obtain the following result.

```
The result of 1st system is :  {z: 3, y: 2, x: 1}
The result of 2nd system is :  {y: 10, x: 5}
```

◀

12.1.2 Limits

To solve limit problems, **limit()** function is used.

Example 12.4 Write a code to find the solutions of the following limits. $y1 = \lim_{x \to \infty}(\frac{\sin 5x}{x})$, and $y2 = \lim_{x \to 0^+}(\frac{1}{x})$

Solution. The following code may be used to accomplish the task.

```
#Example 12.4
#This example finds limit of a function
from sympy import *
x, y = symbols('x y') #y is not used in this example
y1 = limit(sin(5*x)/x, x, 0)
y2 = limit(1/x, x, 0, '+')
print('First Result is :', y1)
print('Second Result is :', y2)
```

Listing 12.4: Example12p4.py

Once the code runs, we will get the following result.

```
First Result is : 5
Second Result is : oo
```

◀

In the output above, "*oo*" represents infinity in the sympy module.

12.1.3 Derivatives

In order to take the derivative of a function, **diff()** function is used.

Example 12.5 Write a code that calculates the first and third derivatives (y' and y''') of $y = 3x^3 - 5x - 20$.

Solution. The following code can be used to accomplish the task.

```
#Example 12.5
#This example finds derivative
from sympy import *
x = Symbol('x')
y = 3*x**3 - 5*x -20
yp = diff(y, x)
yppp = diff(y, x, 3)
print("First derivative is : ", yp)
print("Third derivative is : ", yppp)
```

Listing 12.5: Example12p5.py

Once the code runs, we will obtain the following result.

```
First derivative is :  9*x**2 - 5
Third derivative is :  18
```

◀

12.1.4 Integrals

In order to solve integrals, the **integral()** function is used.

Example 12.6 Write a code to calculate $y1$ and $y2$ in the following integrals: $y1 = \int \tan(x)dx$, and $y2 = \int_{-\infty}^{\infty} \int_{-\infty}^{\infty} e^{-x^2-y^2} dxdy$

Solution. The following code can be used to accomplish the task.

```
#Example 12.6
#This example calculates integrals
from sympy import *
x, y = symbols('x y')
Firsty = tan(x)
```

```
Secondy = exp(-x**2-y**2)
y1 = integrate(Firsty , x)
y2 = integrate(Secondy, (x, -oo, oo), (y, -oo, oo))
print("y1 is : ", y1)
print("y2 is : ", y2)
```

Listing 12.6: Example12p6.py

As can be seen in the code above, *'oo'* is used to represent infinity for the range of $y2$. Once the code runs, we will obtain the following result.

```
y1 is :  -log(sin(x)**2 - 1)/2
y2 is :  pi
```

◄

12.1.5 Ordinary Differential Equations

To solve ordinary differential equations, the **dsolve()** function is used.

Example 12.7 Write a code that calculates the solutions of the equation $y\prime + 3y = 3$

Solution. The following code can be used to accomplish the task.

```
#Example 12.7
#This example solves an ODE with dsolve
from sympy import *
x = Symbol('x')
f = Function('f') # y is f
Result = dsolve(Eq(Derivative(f(x),x) + 3*f(x), 3),f(x))
print(Result)
```

Listing 12.7: Example12p7.py

Once the code runs, we will obtain the following result.

```
Eq(f(x), C1*exp(-3*x) + 1)
```

◄

Therefore, it will be seen that the solution is $y = C_1 e^{-3x} + 1$.

Example 12.8 Write a code that calculates the solutions of the equation $y\prime\prime + y = 2$

Solution. The following code may be used to accomplish the task.

```
#Example 12.8
#This example solves an ODE with dsolve
from sympy import *
x = Symbol('x')
f = Function('f') # y is f
Result = dsolve(Eq(Derivative(f(x),x,x) + f(x), 2),f(x))
print(Result)
```

Listing 12.8: Example12p8.py

Once the code runs, we will obtain the following result.

```
Eq(f(x), C1*sin(x) + C2*cos(x) + 2)
```

◀

Thus, it will be seen that the solution is $y = C_1 \sin(x) + C_2 \cos(x) + 2$.

12.1.6 Partial Differential Equations

The **pdsolve()** function is used to solve partial differential equations.

Example 12.9 Write a code to solve the equation $3u_x + 2u_y = 0$

Solution. The following code can be used to accomplish the task.

```
#Example 12.9
#This example solves a pde
from sympy.solvers.pde import pdsolve
from sympy import Function, diff, Eq
from sympy.abc import x, y
f = Function('f')
u = f(x, y)
ux = u.diff(x)
uy = u.diff(y)
eq = Eq(3*ux + 2*uy)
Result = pdsolve(eq)
print(Result)
```

Listing 12.9: Example12p9.py

Once the code runs, we will get the following result.

```
Eq(f(x, y), F(2*x - 3*y))
```

◀

12.2 Evaluating Equations or Expressions

The **evalf()** function is used to evaluate a function at a point.

Example 12.10 Write a code that evaluates $y1(3.14)$ and $y2(\frac{\pi}{4})$ where $y1 = \frac{\sin(x)}{x}$, $y2 = \sin(x) + \cos(x)$.

Solution. The following code may be used to accomplish the task.

```
#Example 12.10
#This example evaluates value
from math import pi as pi
from sympy import *
from sympy.abc import x
y1 = sin(x)/x
y2 = sin(x) + cos(x)
Result1 = y1.evalf(subs = {x:3.14})
Result2 = y2.evalf(subs = {x:pi/4})
print(Result1)
print(Result2)
```

Listing 12.10: Example12p10.py

Once the code runs, we will obtain the following result.

```
0.000507214304613640
1.41421356237310
```

◀

12.3 PROBLEMS

12.1 Consider the following algebraic equation:

$$y = \frac{(x-2)(x-3)}{x^2-9}$$

Write a code that prints the given algebraic equation in its simplest form on the screen.

12.2 Write a code to solve $y = x^2 + 2x - 8$.

12.3 Write a code to solve the following system of equations.

$$\begin{cases} 2x + y = 1 \\ -5x + 2y = -7 \end{cases}$$

12.4 Write a code to find the solution of the following limit:

$$y = \lim_{x \to 0} (\frac{\sin(6x)}{18x})$$

12.5 Write a code that calculates the second derivative (y'') of $y = 5x^2 - 10x - 2017$.

12.6 Write a code that calculates the solution to the integral

$$y = \int_0^{20} \int_0^{10} 5y dx dy$$

12.7 Write a code to calculate the solution of $y\prime\prime + y = 0$.

12.8 Write a code to solve $-2u_x + 2u_y = 1$

12.9 Write a code to evaluate $y(\frac{\pi}{6})$ where $y = 2\sin(x) + 3\cos(x)$.

12.10 Write a code to evaluate $y(\frac{\pi}{4})$ where $y = 2\sin(2x) - 3\cos(4x)$.

Chapter 13

INTRODUCTION TO STATISTICS

Python provides a wide range of functions accompanying its modules related to statistical applications.

In this chapter, we will introduce some introductory topics. First, we will take a look at statistical built-in functions. Then, functions being used in random number generators will be considered. Finally, some built-in functions that are commonly used in distributions will be overviewed.

For some the examples, you may need to have **simpy**, **statistics** or **stats** modules.

13.1 Basic Statistical Functions

We can calculate some of the basic parameters by using the built-in functions available in the modules mentioned above. By defining functions, same, as well as different parameters can be calculated. But to keep it simple, we will only consider the parameters that are commonly used with functions that come with the modules.

Table 13.1: Some of the available functions related to statistical applications

Function	Description
mean()	calculates the arithmetic mean (average) of data
median()	calculates the median of data
median_low()	calculates the low median of data
median_high()	calculates the high median of data
mode()	calculates the mode most repeating number of data
pstdev()	calculates the population standard deviation of data
pvariance()	calculates the population variance of data
stdev()	calculates the sample standard deviation of data
variance()	calculates the sample variance of data

Example 13.1 In a class, heights of the students are given as H = [156, 162, 180, 160, 178, 175, 182, 170, 175, 190] in centimeters. Using these data, write a code to calculate the mean, median, mode, population variance, and the sample standard deviation of the data.

Solution. The following code may be used to calculate these values.

```
#Example 13.1
#This example finds statistical values
import statistics as st
H = [156, 162, 180, 160, 178, 175, 182, 170, 175, 190]
Mean = st.mean(H)
Median = st.median(H)
Mode = st.mode(H)
PopVar = st.pvariance(data=H, mu=Mean)
SampleStDev = st.stdev(H)
print("Mean of H is : ", Mean)
print("Median of H is : ", Median)
print("Mode of H is : ", Mode)
print("Population variance of H is : ", PopVar)
```

```
print("Sample standard deviation of H is : ", SampleStDev)
```

Listing 13.1: Example13p1.py

Once the code runs, we will get the following result.

```
Mean of H is :  172.8
Median of H is :  175.0
Mode of H is :  175
Population variance of H is :  103.96000000000001
Sample standard deviation of H is :  10.747609553343064
```

◀

13.2 Random Number Generators

There are various number generators being used in Python. Some of these generators are listed in Table 13.2.

Table 13.2: Some of used random number generator functions

Function	Description
numpy.random. rand(A,B)	creates an A by B array filled with random numbers from uniform distribution over [0,1)
numpy.random. randn(A,B)	creates an A by B array filled with random numbers from normal distribution with mean of 0 and variance of 1
numpy.random. randint(A,B,N)	creates N number of random integers from discrete uniform distribution over [A,B)
numpy.random. random_sample((A,B))	creates an A by B array filled with random numbers from continuous uniform distribution over [0,1)

Example 13.2 Write a code that employs all the functions listed above, to pick randomly selected numbers. The size of the numbers should be 2 by 4 for all functions except the **randint()** function, which has to pick 20 numbers between 1 and 6.

Solution. The code can be written as follows.

```
#Example 13.2
#This example picks randomly numbers
import numpy.random as nr
x = nr.rand(2,4)
y = nr.randn(2,4)
z= nr.randint(1,7,20)#20 numbers between 1 and 6
t= nr.random_sample((2,4)) # watch out for 2 double parentheses
print("By using rand(2,4) :\n", x)
print("By using randn(2,4) :\n", y)
print("By using randint(1,7,20) :\n", z)
print("By using random_sample(2,4) :\n", t)
```

Listing 13.2: Example13p2.py

Once the code runs, we will obtain the following output.

```
By using rand(2,4) :
 [[ 0.45424086  0.5961028   0.26616812  0.62368451]
 [ 0.07308653  0.41037998  0.01437008  0.37256405]]
By using randn(2,4) :
 [[-1.27684843 -0.44630039  0.20568888 -0.79596624]
 [-0.26786607  1.44272394 -0.59504564 -0.88544482]]
By using randint(1,7,20) :
 [4 2 6 4 4 6 2 3 1 2 2 6 4 3 3 6 5 2 1 6]
By using random_sample((2,4)) :
 [[ 0.48667912  0.26908029  0.01141098  0.54464949]
 [ 0.05861147  0.66660083  0.25191056  0.87214736]]
```

◀

13.3 Distributions

There are various distribution functions available in the scipy module. A few of them are shown in the table below.

Table 13.3: Some of distribution functions in the **scipy.stats** module

Distribution Name	Function	Explanation
Beta	beta(A, B)	A and B are the shape parameters
Binomial	binom(S,P)	S stands for size and P stands for probability
Chi-squared	chi2(DF)	DF stands for the density function
Exponential	expon	Values for the sample are passed to function
Normal	norm(loc, scale)	Loc specifies the mean, scale specifies the standard deviation
Poisson	poisson(mu)	mu is the shape parameter
Uniform	uniform(A,B)	A and B are the passed parameters

Example 13.3 Write a code to calculate values for Beta-distribution where alpha and beta parameters are $[0.5, 1, 2]$ and $[0.5, 1, 3]$, respectively, for 1000 values between 0 and 1. The results are expected to be shown on a plot.

Solution. The following code can be used to accomplish the task.

```
#Example 13.3
#Example for a Beta distribution
import numpy as np
from scipy.stats import beta
from matplotlib import pyplot as plt
#distribution parameters
alpha_v = [0.5, 1.0, 2.0]
beta_v = [0.5, 1.0, 3.0]
x = np.linspace(0, 1, 1000)
for shape1, shape2, in zip(alpha_v, beta_v):
#zip function aggregates the elements from each list
    distribut = beta(shape1, shape2)
    plt.plot(x,distribut.pdf(x))
```

```
#plotting the result of the probability density function (pdf)
# for the object of beta distribution
plt.legend(["alpha=0.5 | beta=0.5",
"alpha=1.0 | beta=1.0", "alpha=2.0 | beta=3.0"])
plt.title('Beta')
plt.show()
```

Listing 13.3: Example13p3.py

Once the code is run, the following output is obtained.

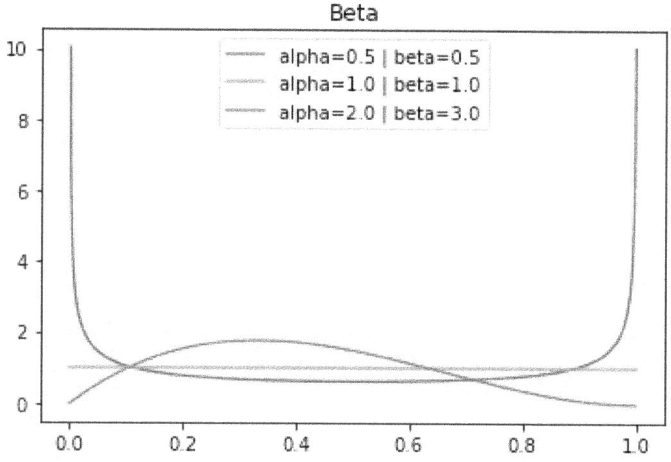

Figure 13.1: Plot of a Beta-distribution

◀

Example 13.4 Write a code to plot the graph of a normal distribution (bell curve), where the mean value is 5 and the variance is equal to 1.

Solution. We can generate 100 numbers between 2 and 8 where the mean value is 5. The code can be written as follows.

```
#Example 13.4
#Example for a Normal distribution
import matplotlib.pyplot as plt
import numpy as np
```

```
import math
from scipy import stats
mu = 5 # mean
variance = 1
sigma = math.sqrt(variance)
NormalDist = stats.norm(loc=mu, scale = sigma)
# Above, loc = mean, scale = standard deviation
x = np.linspace(2, 8, 100)
y = NormalDist.pdf(x) #pdf stands for probability density function
plt.plot(x,y)
plt.grid(True) # grid on
plt.ylabel('y')
plt.xlabel('Mean is 5')
plt.title('Graph of A Normal Distribution')
plt.show()
```

Listing 13.4: Example13p4.py

Once the code runs, we will obtain the following output.

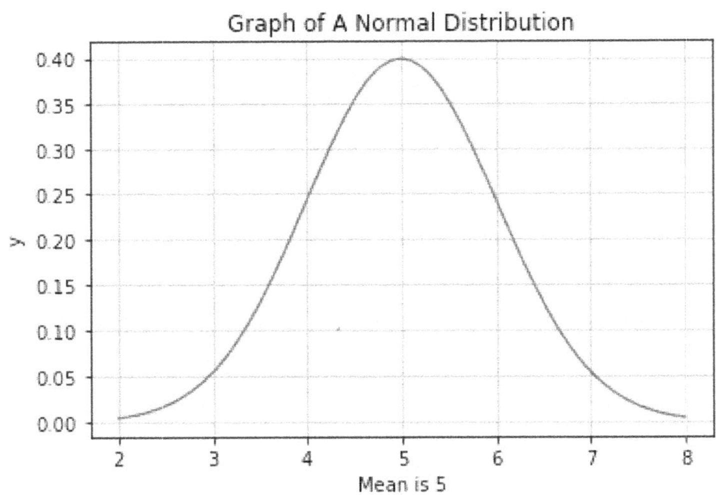

Figure 13.2: Graph of a Normal distribution

◀

Example 13.5 Write a code to calculate the values for a Poisson distribution for

[5, 10, 20] values over the range [0, 50].

Solution. The following code may be used to accomplish the task.

```
#Example 13.5
#Example for a Poisson distribution
import numpy as np
from scipy.stats import poisson
from matplotlib import pyplot as plt
#distribution parameters
mu_val = [5, 10, 20]
x = np.arange(0,51)
for mu in mu_val:
    distribut = poisson(mu)
    plt.plot(x,distribut.pmf(x))
#plotting the result of the probability mass function (pmf)
# for the object of poisson distribution
plt.legend(["mu=5", "mu=10", "mu=20"])
plt.title('Poisson')
plt.show()
```

Listing 13.5: Example13p5.py

Once the code runs, the following output will be obtained.

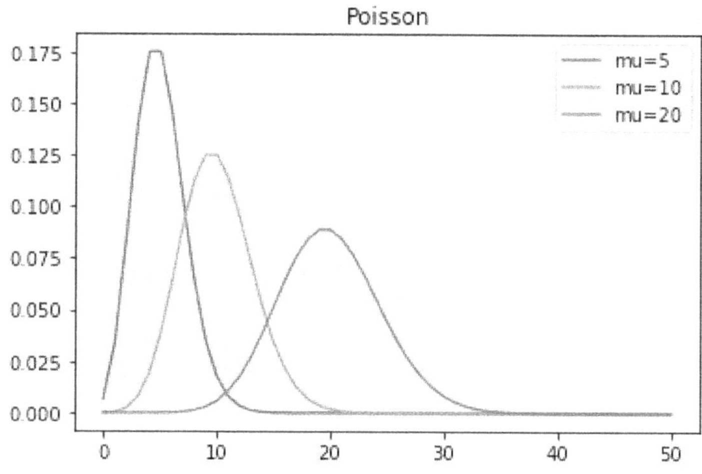

Figure 13.3: Graph of a Poisson distribution

◀

13.4 PROBLEMS

13.1 In a class, weights of the students are given as H = [65, 78, 80, 160, 100, 75, 78] in kilograms. By using the given data, write a code to calculate the mean, median, mode, population variance, and the sample standard deviation of the data.
13.2 Write a code that randomly picks numbers using the **rand()** and **randn()** functions. The size of the array of numbers should be 4 by 5.
13.3 Write a code that calculates the values for a Beta distribution where the alpha and beta parameters are [2, 4] and [1, 3], respectively, for 500 values between 0 and 1. The results are expected to be shown on a graph.
13.4 Write a code to plot the graph of a normal distribution (bell curve), where the mean value is 10 and the variance is equal to 1.
13.5 Write a code to calculate the values for a Poisson distribution for [3, 5] values over the range [0, 20].

Chapter 14

NUMERICAL METHODS

In this chapter, we will introduce the following topics: Interpolation, Curve Fitting, Root Finding, Numerical Differentiation, Numerical Integration, and Ordinary Differential Equations from a numerical methods perspective.

Before we start examining these techniques, it is important to talk about the decimal module and the accuracy of its results. When the numbers are used via the decimal module, the results become more accurate with the help of fast and correctly rounded floating point calculations. In order to show the benefits of using the decimal module, we may take a look at the following example.

Example 14.1 Write a code about the accuracy of the results. The code must show the difference between whether you use the decimal module or not for the calculation of $0.1 + 0.1 + 0.1 - 0.3$.

Solution. The following code can be used to accomplish the task.

```
#Example 14.1
#This example shows using the decimal module
from decimal import Decimal as D
#for accuracy, use decimal module
Decim  =  D(0) + D("0.1") + D("0.1") + D("0.1") - D("0.3")
Normal =  0.1 + 0.1 + 0.1 - 0.3
print("Result with Decimal Calculation :", Decim)
print("Result with Normal Calculation  :", Normal)
```

Listing 14.1: Example14p1.py

Once the code runs, we will get the following result.

```
Result with Decimal Calculation : 0.0
Result with Normal Calculation  : 5.551115123125783e-17
```

◀

It is obvious that, using the decimal module improves the precision of the calculated results.

14.1 Interpolation

We can find a corresponding value of a point within a given domain by using the **interp()** function in **numpy** module. The function works for 1-dimensional linear interpolation.

Example 14.2 Write a code to find the corresponding value of 2.2 by using the given pairs of points $(0.0, 0.0), (1.0, 0.5), (1.5, 0.8), (2.0, -0.3), (2.5, 1.0)$, and $(3.5, 2.0)$.

Solution. We can use the **interp()** function in **numpy** module to accomplish the given task.

```
#Example 14.2
#This example uses interpolation
import numpy as np
x_valeus = [0.0, 1.0, 1.5, 2.0,  2.5,  3.5]
y_values = [0.0, 0.5, 0.8, -0.3, 1.0, 2.0]
x = np.array(x_valeus)
y = np.array(y_values)
Correspond = np.interp(2.2, x, y)
print("Value Corresponding to 2.2  is :\n", Correspond)
```

Listing 14.2: Example14p2.py

As can be seen from the code, the domain is [0.0, 3.5]. And 2.2 is between 0.0 and 3.5.

Once the code runs, we will obtain the following result.

```
Value Corresponding to 2.2  is :
 0.22000000000000047
```

◀

14.2 Curve Fitting

We can fit polynomial functions to a set of data by using the **polyfit()** function within the numpy module. Then by using the **poly1d()** function again in numpy module, the polynomial is created and the function can be evaluated at any point for 1-dimensional applications.

In other words, the coefficients of a polynomial function such as $p(x) = a_n x^n + a_{n-1}x^{n-1} + ... + a_1 x + a_0$ having a degree of n are created using (x_0, y_0),(x_1, y_1),...,(x_k, y_k), with $k+1$ points. Then the function is created and evaluated at any given point.

Example 14.3 Write a code to find the coefficients of the polynomial function for the pairs of points (0.0, 0.0), (1.0, 0.5), (1.5, 0.8), (2.0, -0.3), (2.5, 1.0), and (3.5, 2.0). Then, the code is expected to print out the function and value of the function at x = 10.

Solution. The following code may be used to accomplish the task.

```
#Example 14.3
#This example creates a polynomial
#  and evaluates a value in it
import numpy as np
x_valeus = [0.0, 1.0, 1.5, 2.0,  2.5,  3.5]
y_values = [0.0, 0.5, 0.8, -0.3, 1.0, 2.0]
x = np.array(x_valeus)
y = np.array(y_values)
z = np.polyfit(x, y, deg=3)
print("Coefficients of polynomial are :\n",z)
p = np.poly1d(z)
print("The polynomial function is :\n", p)
print("Value of the function at x = 10 is :", p(10))
```

Listing 14.3: Example14p3.py

Once the code runs, the following result will be obtained.

```
Coefficients of polynomial are :
 [ 0.21293952 -0.91631959  1.17877819  0.02099496]
The polynomial function is :
         3          2
```

```
0.2129 x - 0.9163 x + 1.179 x + 0.02099
Value of the function at x = 10 is : 133.116340003
```

◀

14.3 Root Finding

In order to find roots of functions as scalar values, **scipy.optimize** sub-package can be used. To evaluate a function at a point, the function should be defined first. The following methods are commonly used in root finding.

14.3.1 Bisection Method

When the bisection method is to be used, the **bisect(function, a, b)** is utilized, which indicates that the root is between a and b. The sign of the function at points a and b must be different.

Example 14.4 Write a code to find the root of the function $f(x) = x^3 - 4x^2 + x + 6$ between -2 and 0 using the bisection method.

Solution. The following code may be used to accomplish the task.

```
#Example 14.4
#This example finds root by using bisection method
from scipy import optimize as op
def funct(x):
    return x**3 - 4*x**2 + x + 6
Root = op.bisect(funct,-2,0)
print("The root is : ", Root)
```

Listing 14.4: Example14p4.py

Once the code runs, we will get the following result.

```
The root is :  -1.0
```

◀

14.3.2 Newton's Method

When we prefer to use Newton's method, the **newton(function,** $x0$**)** function is used within the **scipy.optimize** sub-package where $x0$ is the initial guess.

Example 14.5 Write a code to find the root of the function $f(x) = x^3 - 4x^2 + x + 6$ using Newton's method where the initial guess is equal to 4.

Solution. The following code can be used to accomplish the task.

```
#Example 14.5
#This example finds root by using Newton's method
from scipy import optimize as op
def funct(x):
    return x**3 - 4*x**2 + x + 6
Root = op.newton(funct,4)
print("The root is : ", Root)
```

Listing 14.5: Example14p5.py

Once the code runs, we will obtain the following result.

```
The root is :  3.0000000000000004
```

◀

14.4 Numerical Differentiation

In order to calculate the derivative of a function numerically at a given point, the **derivative()** function in **scipy.misc** module can be used. The function employs the **central difference** formula for approximation. The function takes three parameters as the input, including the defined function, the point where the derivative is evaluated, and the step size or mesh size.

Example 14.6 Write a code that evaluates the numerical derivative of the function given by $f(x) = x^3 + x^2$ at $x = 2$ with the spacing/mesh size $dx = 1 * 10^{-6}$ using the **derivative()** function.

Solution. We already know that, the exact solution to this problem is 16. However, to show how the function works, we can utilize the following code to perform the numerical calculations using the derivative() function.

```
#Example 14.6
#This example uses derivative() function
from scipy.misc import derivative
def f(x):
    return x**3 + x**2
Der = derivative(f, 2.0, dx=1e-6) #evaluate f at x=2 with mesh size dx
print("Result is : ", Der)
```

Listing 14.6: Example14p6.py

Once the code runs, we will obtain the following result.

```
Result is :  16.0000000013
```

◄

As can be seen from the result, the error is equal to $dx = 1.3 * 10^{-9}$

14.5 Numerical Integration

In order to perform numerical integration of functions over an interval (definite integrals), the **quad()** and **romberg()** functions can be used from the **scipy.integrate** sub-package. There are some other functions also available such as dblquad(), tplquad(), nquad(), or fixed_quad() . In this section, however, we will only use the quad() and romberg() functions pertaining to our example.

The **quad()** function takes three parameters: The function, starting point, and the end point, and it returns two parameters: The first being the value of the numerical integration and the second is the error.

Another function that performs the numerical integration is the **romberg()** function, which employs the Romberg method. This function, too, takes three parameters including the function, starting point, and the end point; and returns the result as its mere parameter.

In addition, the function whose integral is to be evaluated must be defined, as well.

Example 14.7 Write a code that finds the numerical solution of $\int_0^2 f(x)dx$ where $f(x) = 3x^2 + 2$ by using the quad() and romberg() functions.

Solution. The following code may be used to accomplish the task.

```
#Example 14.7
#This example calculates numerical integration
from scipy.integrate import quad
from scipy.integrate import romberg
def funct(x):
    return 3*x**2 + 2
NumQuad, Error = quad(funct,0,2)
NumRomb = romberg(funct,0,2)
print("Numerical Integration with quad-function: ", NumQuad)
print("Error with quad function :", Error)
print("Numerical Integration with quad-function: ", NumRomb)
```

Listing 14.7: Example14p7.py

Once the code runs, the following result will be obtained.

```
Numerical Integration with quad-function:  12.0
Error with quad function : 1.3322676295501878e-13
Numerical Integration with quad-function:  12.0
```

◄

14.6 Ordinary Differential Equations

Numerical solutions of ordinary differential equations have important applications in a wide variety of areas in engineering and applied sciences. Python has the **odeint()** function in **scipy.integrate** sub-package that solves the ordinary differential equations with an initial condition.

Ordinary differential equations with initial values can be solved using the Euler and Runge-Kutta methods, too.

In this section, we will show how to solve initial value problems of ordinary differential equations using the odeint() function, Euler method, and 4th Order Runge-Kutta Method.

14.6.1 odeint() Function

Scipy module has the **odeint()** function in scipy.integrate sub-package to solve initial value problems of ordinary differential equations for both stiff and non-stiff problems. This function is used as **scipy.integrate.odeint(dydx, y0, xval)**. It takes three parameters: $dydx$ is the derivative of the function of y with respect to x, $y0$ is the initial value, and $xval$ is the vector of values of x.

Example 14.8 Write a code to solve the following initial value problem given by

$$\frac{dy}{dx} = y - x, \; y(0) = \frac{2}{3}, \; 0 \leq x \leq 5$$

using the **odeint()** function where the exact solution is $y = (x+1) - \frac{1}{3}e^x$. The code should print the solution at $x = 5$ ($y(5)$) on the screen and plot the graphs of the numerical solution and the exact solution on the same figure, besides plotting the error on a separate figure. The mesh size (the interval between each x value) should be chosen as 0.0005.

Solution. The following code may be used to accomplish the given tasks.

```
#Example 14.8
#This example solves a first order ode numerically and plot graphics
from scipy.integrate import odeint
import numpy as np
import matplotlib.pyplot as plt
#defining function of dy/dx
def dy_over_dx(y, x):
    return y - x
xval = np.linspace(0,5,10001) # 0<=x<=5
y0 = 2.0/3.0 #initial condition
yval = odeint(dy_over_dx, y0, xval)
print("Numerical Solution of y(5) : ", yval[10000])
yval = np.array(yval).flatten()
y_exact = xval + 1 - (1.0/3.0)*np.exp(xval)
y_difference = yval - y_exact
plt.plot(xval, yval,"-", xval, y_exact, "+")
plt.xlabel("x")
plt.ylabel("y")
plt.title("Numerical and Analytical Solutions")
plt.legend(["Numerical Solution","Exact Solution"])
```

```
#plotting error in a new figure
plt.figure()
y_diff = np.abs(y_exact - yval)
plt.semilogy(xval, y_diff)
plt.ylabel("Error")
plt.xlabel("x")
plt.title("Error in numerical integration")
plt.show()
```

Listing 14.8: Example14p8.py

Once the code runs, we will get the following output and plots:

```
Numerical Solution of y(5) :  [-43.47105949]
```

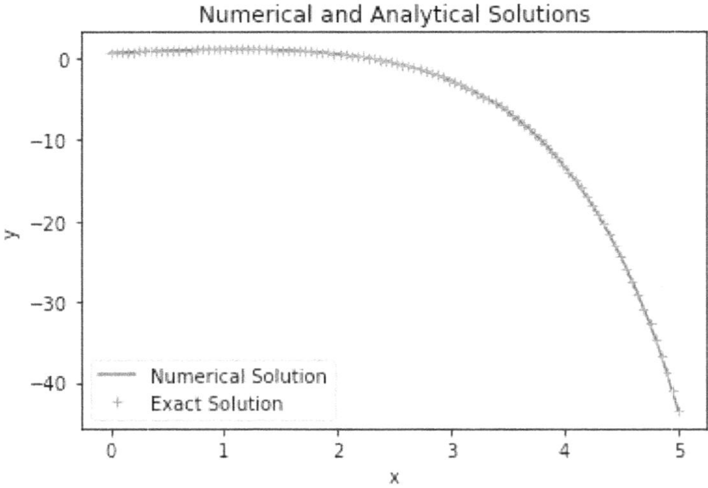

Figure 14.1: Plots of the Numerical and Exact Solutions

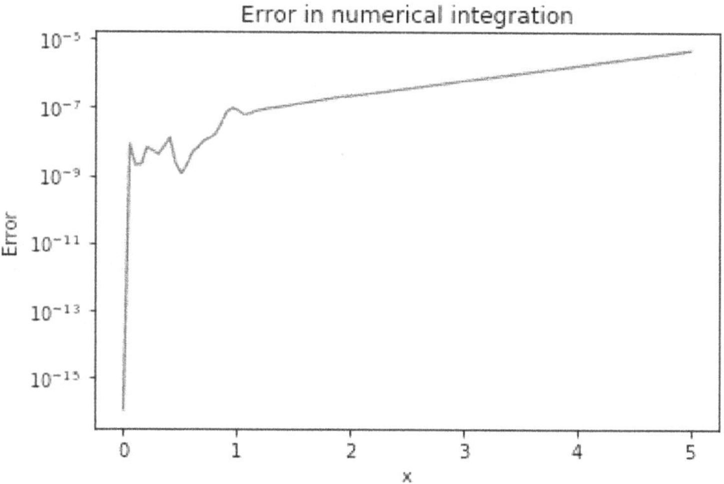

Figure 14.2: Plot of the error in numerical integration

14.6.2 Euler's Method

Euler Method is another way to find approximate solutions to initial value problems of ordinary differential equations of the following type:

$$\begin{cases} \frac{dy}{dx} = f(x, y) \\ y(a) = y_a \end{cases},$$

$$y_{i+1} = y_i + hf(x_i, y_i),$$

where h is the mesh size(in a uniform mesh) over the interval [**a, b**].

Example 14.9 Write a code to solve the initial value problem given by

$$\frac{dy}{dx} = y - x, \, y(0) = \frac{2}{3}, \, 0 \leq x \leq 5$$

using the **Euler Method** where the exact solution is $y = (x + 1) - \frac{1}{3}e^x$ The code should print the exact solution and numerical solution of $y(5)$ on the screen. The mesh size, h, should be chosen as $h = 0.0005$.

Solution. The following code can be used to accomplish the tasks mentioned above.

```
#Example 14.9
#This example solves a first order
#  ode by using Euler Method
import numpy as np
def f(x, y):
    return y - x
y = 2.0/3.0 #initial condition
xval = np.linspace(0,5,10001) # 0<=x<=5
h = xval[1]-xval[0] # h is mesh size and it is uniform
for i in xval:
    y = y + f(i,y)*h # Euler formula
print("Numerical Solution of y(5) : ", y)
y_exact = 5.0 + 1.0 - (1.0/3.0)*np.exp(5.0)
print("Exact Solution of y(5)     : ",y_exact)
```

Listing 14.9: Example14p9.py

Once the code runs, the following results will be obtained.

```
Numerical Solution of y(5) :  -43.4334780673
Exact Solution of y(5)     :  -43.4710530342
```

◀

14.6.3 Runge-Kutta Method of 4th Order

Runge-Kutta Methods comprise another group of methods for solving initial value problems of ordinary differential equations. In this section, we will consider the 4th order (**RK4**) formula, which has the following form:

$$\begin{cases} \frac{dy}{dx} = f(x,y) \\ y(a) = y_a,\ a \le x \le b \end{cases},$$

$$\begin{cases} K_1 = hf(x_i, y_i) \\ K_2 = hf(x_i + \frac{1}{2}h, y_i + \frac{1}{2}K_1 h) \\ K_3 = hf(x_i + \frac{1}{2}h, y_i + \frac{1}{2}K_2 h) \\ K_4 = hf(x_i + h, y_i + K_3 h) \\ y_{i+1} = y_i + \frac{1}{6}(K_1 + 2K_2 + 2K_3 + K_4) \end{cases},$$

Example 14.10 Write a code to solve the initial value problem given by

$$\frac{dy}{dx} = y - x, \, y(0) = \frac{2}{3}, \, 0 \leq x \leq 5$$

using **RK4**, where the exact solution is $y = (x+1) - \frac{1}{3}e^{x}$ The code should print the exact solution and numerical solution of $y(5)$ on the screen. The mesh size (h) should be chosen as $h = 0.0005$.

Solution. We can write the following code to accomplish the given tasks.

```
#Example 14.10
#This example solves a first order ode
# by using Runge-Kutta Method of 4th order
import numpy as np
def f(x, y):
    return y - x
y = 2.0/3.0 #initial condition
xval = np.linspace(0,5,10001) # 0<=x<=5
h = xval[1]-xval[0] # h is mesh size and it is uniform
for i in xval:
    K1 = h*f(i,y)
    K2 = h*f(i + 0.5*h, y + 0.5*K1*h)
    K3 = h*f(i + 0.5*h, y + 0.5*K2*h)
    K4 = h*f(i + h, y + K3*h)
    y = y + (1.0/6.0)*(K1 + 2.0*K2 + 2.0*K3 + K4) # Runge-Kutta4 formula
print("Numerical Solution of y(5) : ", y)
y_exact = 5.0 + 1.0 - (1.0/3.0)*np.exp(5.0)
print("Exact Solution of y(5)     : ",y_exact)
```

Listing 14.10: Example14p10.py

Once the code runs, we will obtain the following result.

```
Numerical Solution of y(5) :  -43.4703160436
Exact Solution of y(5)     :  -43.4710530342
```

◀

As can be seen from the results, we obtained better results from the 4th-order Runge-Kutta method compared to the results obtained by the Euler method.

14.7 PROBLEMS

14.1 Write a code pertaining to the accuracy of the results. The code is expected to show the difference between using and not using the decimal module for a calculation you picked.
14.2 Write a code to find the corresponding value of 2.4 using the given pairs of points (0.0, 0.0), (1.2, 0.8), (1.9, 0.9), (2.0, 2.0), and (3.3, 2.8).
14.3 Write a code to find the coefficients of the polynomial function for the pairs of points (0.0, 0.0), (0.5, 0.8), (1.1, 0.5), (2.3, -0.8), and (2.1, 1.5). Then, the code should print the function and the value of the function for x = 30.
14.4 Write a code to find the root of the function $f(x) = x^3 + x^2 - 10x + 8$ between -2 and -5 by using the Bisection method.
14.5 Write a code to find the root of the function $f(x) = x^3+x^2-10x+8$ using Newton's method where the initial guess is equal to 0.
14.6 Write a code to evaluate the numerical derivative of the function $f(x) = 2x^4 - x^3$ at $x = 1$ with a spacing/mesh size of $dx = 1 * 10^{-6}$ using the **derivative()** function.
14.7 Write a code to calculate the numerical value of $\int_1^3 f(x)dx$ where $f(x) = 4x^3 + 2x$ using the **quad()** function.
14.8 Write a code to calculate the numerical value of $\int_1^3 f(x)dx$ where $f(x) = 4x^3 + 2x$ using the **romberg()** function.
14.9 Write a code to solve the initial value problem given by

$$\frac{dy}{dx} = y - x - 2,\ y(0) = \frac{8}{3},\ 0 \leq x \leq 4$$

using the **odeint()** function, where the exact solution is $y = (x+1) - \frac{1}{3}e^x$ The code should print the solution at x=4 (y(4)) on the screen and plot the graphs of the numerical and exact solutions on the same figure besides plotting the error on a separate figure. The mesh size (the interval between each x value) should be chosen as 0.001.
14.10 Write a code to solve the initial value problem given by

$$\frac{dy}{dx} = y - x - 2,\ y(0) = \frac{8}{3},\ 0 \leq x \leq 4$$

using the **Euler Method**, where the exact solution is $y = (x+1) - \frac{1}{3}e^x$. The code should print the exact and numerical solutions of y(4) on the screen. The mesh size (h) should be chosen as $h = 0.001$.

14.11 Write a code to solve the initial value problem given by

$$\frac{dy}{dx} = y - x - 2,\ y(0) = \frac{8}{3},\ 0 \leq x \leq 4$$

using the **Runge-Kutta** 4th **Order** method where the exact solution is $y = (x+1) - \frac{1}{3}e^{x}$. The code should print the exact and numerical solutions of y(4) on the screen. The mesh size (h) should be chosen as $h = 0.001$.

Chapter 15

DIGITAL IMAGE PROCESSING

In this chapter, we will present how to use the image tools within Python Image Library and the Scipy module.

Python Image Library (known as PIL) provides many powerful tools and features to work with graphics and image files. The most recent version of PIL is called PILLOW (PIL fork). In this chapter, final version of the PILLOW Documentation (4.1.0.dev0) is mostly used as a reference.

15.1 Image Types

There are standard image types, defined as modes, in the final version of PIL as listed in Table 15.1.

PIL utilizes a Cartesian pixel coordinate system starting from the upper left corner with (0, 0). Coordinates are represented as 2-tuples (x,y), where x represents the width and y represents the height in pixels. Rectangles are represented as 4-tuples, where the first two elements represent the upper left corner. Using the **mode** command, one can find out the type of the image and the names of the bands for the image. Regularly used types or modes of images are L (luminance) for grayscale images, RGB images, and CMYK images for printing color images.

Table 15.1: Standard Image modes

Mode	Explanation
1	1 bit pixels for black and white
L	8 bit pixels for black and white
P	8 bit pixels mapped to other mode using color palette
RGB	3 x 8 bit pixels for true color, Red-Green-Blue
RGBA	4 x 8 bit pixels for true color transparency mask
CMYK	3 x 8 bit pixels for color separation, Cyan-Magenta-Yellow-Black
YCbCr	3 x 8 bit pixels for color video format, referring to JPEG
LAB	3 x 8 bit pixels for L*A*B color space
HSV	3 x 8 bit pixels for Hue-Saturation-Value color space
I	32 bit signed integer pixels
F	32 bit floating point pixels

Table 15.2: Basic functions (or attributes) available in Python

Mode	Explanation
open	loads images from a file
show	displays the loaded images
mode	displays the type of the image
format	displays the format of the images such as jpeg, png,..etc
size	It displays the size of images

Basic functions that are used with images are shown in the table above.

Example 15.1 Write a code that opens the image file "lake1.jpg" from the directory.

Then, display the size, format, and mode of the image on the screen.

Solution. The following code may be used to accomplish the given tasks.

```
#Example 15.1
#This example displays some features
# of an image and image itself
from PIL import Image
img = Image.open("cowboys.png")
print("The size of the image : ", img.size)
print("The format of the image : ", img.format)
print("The type of the image : ", img.mode)
img.show()
```

Listing 15.1: Example15p1.py

Once the code runs, we will obtain the following result.

```
The size of the image :  (605, 356)
The format of the image :  PNG
The type of the image :  RGBA
```

The picture is opened by the computer's default image viewer program as shown in Figure 15.1.

Figure 15.1: The image displayed after running the code in Example 15.1

◀

Once the picture is opened, name of the picture appears to be different than the original one. The reason is that the picture is shown from a temporarily used file.

15.2 Converting Image Formats

There exist many supported image formats categorized as fully supported, read only, write only and identified only.

In order to change the format of an image, **save()** method is used to save the image as in the aimed format.

Example 15.2 Write a code that changes the format of the image "face.png" into .tiff format.

Solution. We can use the following code for the given task.

```
#Example 15.2
#This example shows how to change
#  the format of an image
from PIL import Image
img = Image.open("face.png")
img.save('Test.tiff')
```

Listing 15.2: Example15p2.py

Once the code runs, we will see that the Test.tiff image file is created in the directory.

Figure 15.2: A snapshot from the directory of the saved image

◀

15.3 Manipulating Regions and Bands within an Image

We can cut, paste, merge, or resize some regions within an image.

Table 15.3: Some of the possible operations on images in PIL

Function	Description
crop	cuts a piece from an image
paste	pastes a region onto an image
merge	combines the bands from images
resize	changes the size of images
rotate	rotates the images on the counter-clockwise direction
transpose	transposes the images
convert	converts the modes of images between them
split	splits bands from the image

Example 15.3 Write a code that handles two images. The code should crop a region from the first image, and then, rotate the cropped region by 270 degree and paste it to the left side of the second image. After that, the same cropped region should be flipped from left to right and be pasted to the right side of the second image as a second region.

Solution. The following code may be used to accomplish the given tasks.

```
#Example 15.3
#This example shows how to crop, paste, rotate images
from PIL import Image
fir_img = Image.open("cowboys.png")
sec_img = Image.open("baboon.png")
Region1 = (200,50,400,250)#(left, upper, right, lower)
Region2 = (20,100,220,300)#(left, upper, right, lower)
Region3 = (300,100,500,300)#(left, upper, right, lower)
CroppedImg = fir_img.crop(Region1) # crop Region1 from img
NewImg = CroppedImg.transpose(Image.ROTATE_270)
```

```
sec_img.paste(NewImg, Region2)
RotateAgain = CroppedImg.transpose(Image.FLIP_LEFT_RIGHT)
sec_img.paste(RotateAgain, Region3)
sec_img.save('MyNewImage.png')
sec_img.show()
```

Listing 15.3: Example15p3.py

Once the code runs, the "second_img" will be saved as "MyNewImage.png" into the directory, and we will obtain the following output.

Figure 15.3: The image being displayed after running the code in Example 15.3

◀

Example 15.4 Write a code that splits the bands R, G, and B as r1, g1, and b1. The code should then merge the bands as b1, r1, and g1; and mode the image as RGB. The final version of the image should be saved as "Banding.png" into the directory.

Solution. We can use the following code to accomplish the given tasks.

```
#Example 15.4
#This example shows how to split and merge
from PIL import Image
img = Image.open("baboon.png")
print("The size of the image : ", img.size)
print("The format of the image : ", img.format)
print("The type of the image : ", img.mode)
r1, g1, b1 = img.split()
NewImg = Image.merge('RGB', (b1, r1, g1))
NewImg.save("Banding.png")
NewImg.show()
```

Listing 15.4: Example15p4.py

Once the code runs, we will obtain the following output.

Figure 15.4: Shown image after running Example 15.4

◀

15.4 Converting Image Modes

PIL library supports converting modes between "L" and "RGB" and the standard supported modes. In order to convert between other modes, you may have to use extra steps such as first converting to "RGB", and then to the other mode being aimed.

Example 15.5 Write a code to convert the mode of the image saved from the previous example "Banding.png" from "RGB" to "L".

Solution. We can use the following code for this example.

```
#Example 15.5
#This example shows changing mode
from PIL import Image
img = Image.open("Banding.png").convert('L')
print("Mode of Banding.png : ", img.mode)
img.save("ModeL.png")
img.show()
```

Listing 15.5: Example15p5.py

Once the code runs, we will get the following result.

```
Mode of Banding.png :  L
```

And the image pops up as below.

Figure 15.5: The image displayed after running the code in Example 15.5

◀

15.5 Working with pixels

To play around with pixels, you may make use of some of the functions shown in Table 15.4.

Table 15.4: Some of the useful functions for pixel operations available in PIL

Function	Description
Image.getbands()	displays the name of the each band in a tuple
list(Image.getdata())	displays pixel values of Image as a list
Image.getpixel((x,y))	displays the pixel values at x,y
Image.histogram()	returns a list of pixel counts
Image.point(lambda i: E)	manipulates the pixel values considering E

Example 15.6 Write a code that opens the file "baboon.png". Then, by making use of the **getdata()**, **getpixel()** and **getbands()** functions, your code should display the first three pixel values, the first pixel values and names of the bands of the image, respectively.

Solution. The following code may be used to accomplish the given tasks.

```
#Example 15.6
#This example shows example usages
# of getdata(), getpixel(), and getbands()
from PIL import Image
img = Image.open("baboon.png")
pixels1 = list(img.getdata())
pixel = img.getpixel((0,0))
Bands = img.getbands()
print("The first three pixels are : \n", pixels1[0:3])
print("The first pixel is : \n", pixel)
```

```
print("The Bands are : ", Bands)
```

Listing 15.6: Example15p6.py

Once the code runs, the following results will be obtained.

```
The first three pixels are :
 [(164, 150, 71), (63, 57, 31), (75, 43, 10)]
The first pixel is :
 (164, 150, 71)
The Bands are :  ('R', 'G', 'B')
```

◀

Example 15.7 Write a code to manipulate the bands of the image "baboon.png". The code should check whether or not the image mode is RGB. If not, the code should convert the mode to RGB. Then, for the "R" band, the code should assign 50 to all values. For the "G" band, the code should add 10 to each existing value. And finally, for the "B" band, the code should decrease each existing value by 30%. The code should combine each band to make the layers an "RGB" image and save the image as "ManipulatePixels.png". The final image should be displayed as well.

Solution. We can use the following code to accomplish the given tasks.

```
#Example 15.7
#This example shows how to play
# with pixel values in an RGB image
from PIL import Image
img = Image.open("baboon.png")
if (img.mode != 'RGB'):
    img = img.convert ('RGB')
    print("Mode is converted to RGB")
else:
    print('Yes the mode of the image is already RGB')
pixels1 = list(img.getdata()) # get original pixel values
print("The first four pixels before changing : \n", pixels1[0:4])
Bands = img.split()
R, G, B = 0, 1, 2
out1 = Bands[R].point(lambda i: 50)
```

```
out2 = Bands[G].point(lambda i: i + 10)
out3 = Bands[B].point(lambda i: i*0.70)
img = Image.merge(img.mode, (out1,out2,out3))#combine bands again
pixels1 = list(img.getdata())# get updated pixel values
print("The first four pixels after changing : \n", pixels1[0:4])
img.save("ManipulatePixels.png")
img.show()
```

Listing 15.7: Example15p7.py

Once the code runs, we will get the following printed on the screen.

```
Yes the mode of the image is already RGB
The first four pixels before changing :
 [(164, 150, 71), (63, 57, 31), (75, 43, 10), (95, 94, 46)]
The first four pixels after changing :
 [(5C, 160, 49), (50, 67, 21), (50, 53, 7), (50, 104, 32)]
```

And the image is obtained as shown below. ◄

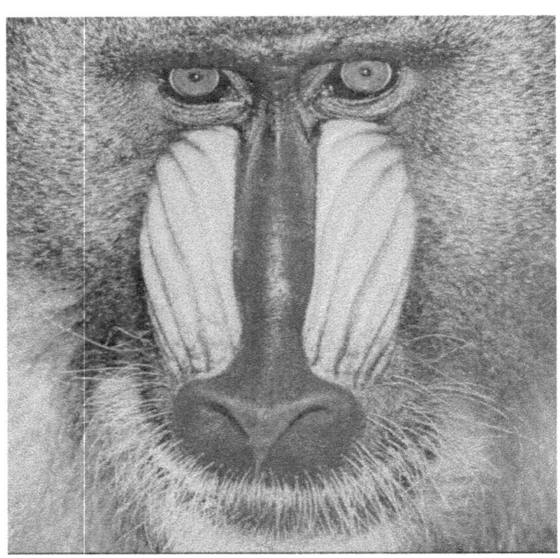

Figure 15.6: The image displayed after running the code in Example 15.7

15.6 Image Filters

In general, filters are used to suppress high frequencies or low frequencies in images. Various filters are available in PIL. To employ filters, the **filter()** function is used.

Table 15.5: Available filters in PIL

BLUR	EMBOSS
CONTOUR	FIND_EDGES
DETAIL	SMOOTH
EDGE_ENHANCE	SMOOTH_MORE
EDGE_ENHANCE_MORE	SHARPEN

Example 15.8 Write a code to use the BLUR, EDGE_ENHANCE_MORE, and SHARPEN filters on the image "baboon.png". The code should display all the filtered images on a single figure.

Solution. The following code may be used to accomplish the given tasks.

```
#Example 15.8
#This example shows some filters
from PIL import Image
from PIL import ImageFilter
import matplotlib.pyplot as plt
img = Image.open("baboon.png")
im = img.copy()#copy original image
img_blur = img.filter(ImageFilter.BLUR)
img_edge_e_m = img.filter(ImageFilter.EDGE_ENHANCE_MORE)
img_sharpen = img.filter(ImageFilter.SHARPEN)
plt.subplot(221)
plt.imshow(im)
plt.title('Original Image')
plt.subplot(222)
plt.imshow(img_blur)
plt.title('Blur Filter')
plt.subplot(223)
```

```
plt.imshow(img_edge_e_m)
plt.title('Edge_Enhance_More Filter')
plt.subplot(224)
plt.imshow(img_sharpen)
plt.title('Sharpen Filter')
plt.show()
```

Listing 15.8: Example15p8.py

Once the code runs, we will obtain the following result.

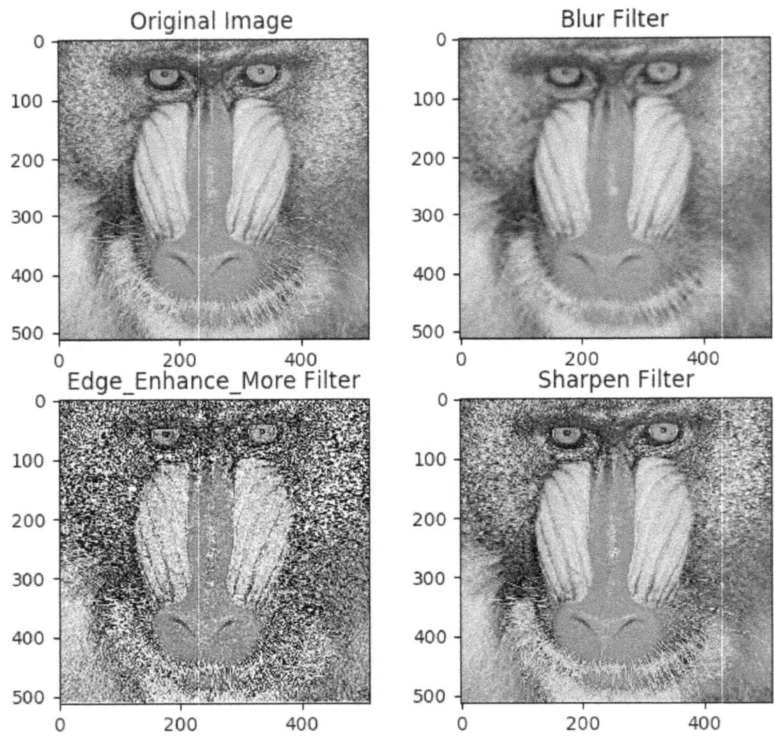

Figure 15.7: The image displayed after running the code in Example 15.8

15.7 Sharpening Images

In order to sharpen images, the "ImageEnhance.Sharpness" class is used.

Example 15.9 Write a code to sharpen the image "baboon.png" with the factors of 0.5, 1.0, 2.0, and 3.0. The code should show all the images on a single figure after sharpening.

Solution. We can use the following code to accomplish the given tasks.

```
#Example 15.9
#This example shown sharpness with different factors
from PIL import Image
from PIL import ImageEnhance
import matplotlib.pyplot as plt
img = Image.open("baboon.png")
Enhancer = ImageEnhance.Sharpness(img)
output1 = Enhancer.enhance(0.5)
plt.subplot(221)
plt.imshow(output1)
plt.title('Sharpness with 0.5')
output2 = Enhancer.enhance(1.0)
plt.subplot(222)
plt.imshow(output2)
plt.title('Sharpness with 1.0')
output3 = Enhancer.enhance(2.0)
plt.subplot(223)
plt.imshow(output3)
plt.title('Sharpness with 2.0')
output4 = Enhancer.enhance(3.0)
plt.subplot(224)
plt.imshow(output4)
plt.title('Sharpness with 3.0')
plt.show()
```

Listing 15.9: Example15p9.py

Once the code runs, we will obtain the following result.

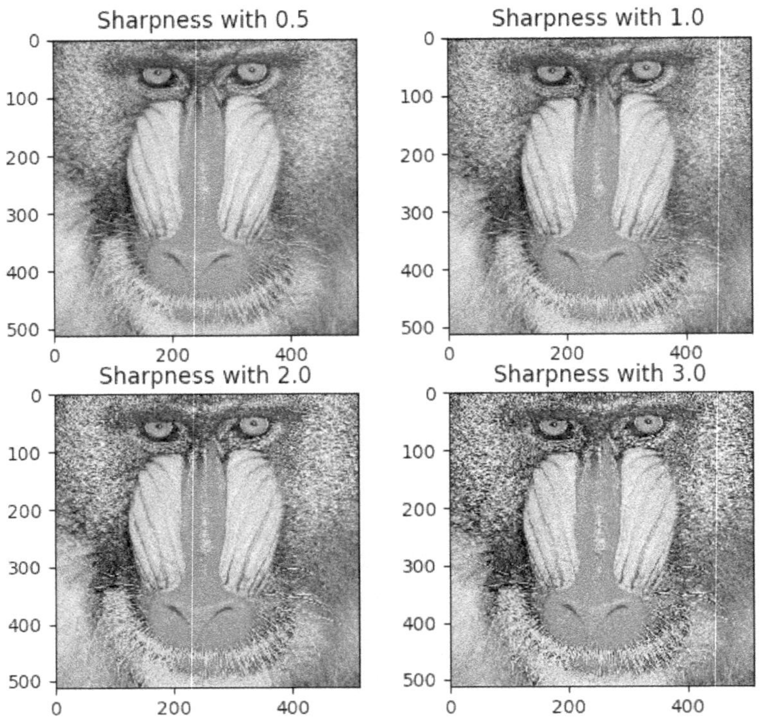

Figure 15.8: The image displayed after running the code in Example 15.9

◀

15.8 Brightening Images

To brighten images, "ImageEnhance.Brightness" class is used.

Example 15.10 Write a code to brighten the image "baboon.png" with the factors of 0.5, 1.0, 2.0, and 3.0. The code should show all the images on a single figure after brightening.

Solution. The following code may be used to accomplish the given tasks.

```
#Example 15.10
#This example shows different brightness with different factors
from PIL import Image
from PIL import ImageEnhance
import matplotlib.pyplot as plt
img = Image.open("baboon.png")
Enhancer = ImageEnhance.Brightness(img)
output1 = Enhancer.enhance(0.5)
plt.subplot(221)
plt.imshow(output1)
plt.title('Brightness with 0.5')
output2 = Enhancer.enhance(0.8)
plt.subplot(222)
plt.imshow(output2)
plt.title('Brightness with 0.8')
output3 = Enhancer.enhance(1.0)
plt.subplot(223)
plt.imshow(output3)
plt.title('Brightness with 1.0')
output4 = Enhancer.enhance(1.5)
plt.subplot(224)
plt.imshow(output4)
plt.title('Brightness with 1.5')
plt.show()
```

Listing 15.10: Example15p10.py

Once the code runs, we will obtain the following result.

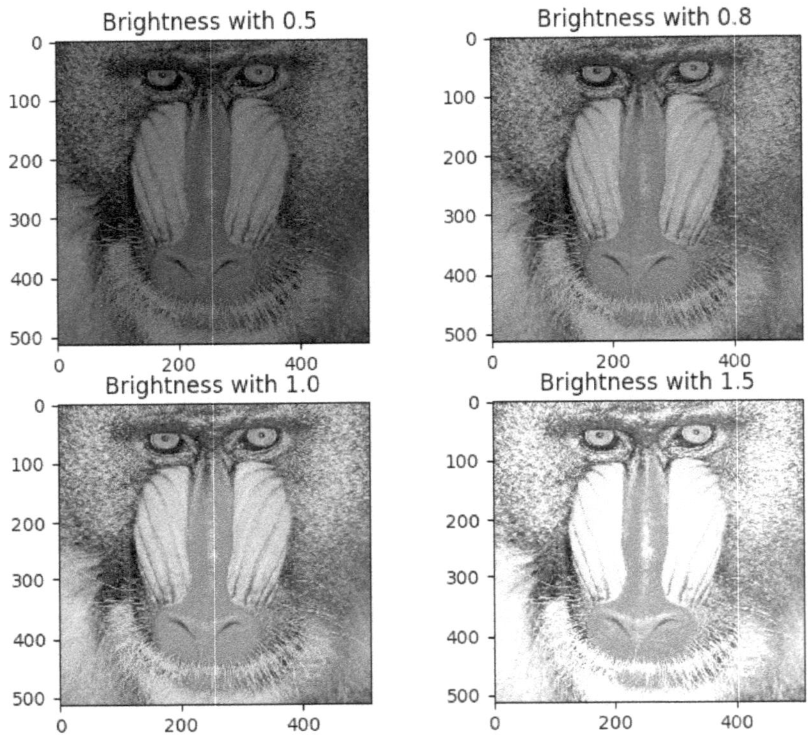

Figure 15.9: The image displayed after running the code in Example 15.10

◀

15.9 Image Operations with Scipy Module

In the scipy module, similar functions and operations are also possible as in PILLOW. Various filters such as Gaussian, Sobel, Prewitt, and Uniform can be used within the scipy module.

Example 15.11 Write a code to apply Gaussian, Sobel, Prewitt, and Uniform filters using the image "face.png" in the scipy module. The code is expected to display all the filtered images on a single figure.

Solution. We can use the following code to accomplish the given tasks.

```
#Example 15.11
#This example shows some filters in scipy.ndimage
from scipy import ndimage as sn
import matplotlib.pyplot as plt
img = sn.imread("face.png")
print("Type :", type(img))#class
print("Shape :", img.shape)#size
print("Data Type :", img.dtype)
gf = sn.gaussian_filter(img, sigma=5)#sigma:scalar or sequence of scalars
sf = sn.sobel(img)
pf = sn.prewitt(img)
uf = sn.uniform_filter(img)
plt.figure(figsize=(15, 15))
plt.subplot(221)
plt.imshow(gf)
plt.title('Gaussian Filter')
plt.subplot(222)
plt.imshow(sf)
plt.title('Sobel Filter')
plt.subplot(223)
plt.imshow(pf)
plt.title('Prewitt Filter')
plt.subplot(224)
plt.imshow(uf)
plt.title('Uniform Filter')
plt.show()
```

Listing 15.11: Example15p11.py

Once the code runs, we will obtain the following results printed on the screen.

```
Type : <class 'numpy.ndarray'>
Shape : (768, 1024, 3)
Data Type : uint8
```

And the resulting image is shown below.

Figure 15.10: The image displayed after running the code in Example 15.11

15.10 PROBLEMS

15.1 Write a code that opens an image from your computer's directory. Then, the code should display the size, format, and mode of the image on the screen.

15.2 Write a code that converts the format of the image being used in the first problem to .png format.

15.3 Write a code that handles two images. The code should crop a square region from the first image. Then, the cropped region should be rotated by 180 degree and be pasted to the left side of the second image.

15.4 Write a code to split the bands R, G, and B as r1, g1, and b1. Then, the code should merge the bands as g1, b1, and r1; and mode the image as RGB. The final version of the image should be saved as "Layers.png" within the directory.

15.5 Write a code that converts the mode of the file "Layers.png" saved in the previous problem from RGB to "L".

15.6 Write a code to apply Gaussian and Uniform filters within the scipy module using an image from your computer's directory. The code should show all the filtered images on a single figure.

15.7 Write a code to manipulate the bands of an RGB image in your directory. The code should check whether or not the mode of the image is RGB. If not, the code should convert the mode to RGB. Then, for the "R" band, the code should add 100 to all existing values. For the "G" band, the code should subtract 10 from each existing value. And finally, for the "B" band, the code should decrease each existing value by 50%. The code should combine each band to make the layers an "RGB" image, and save the image as "New.png". The final image should be displayed as well.

15.8 Write a code to implement CONTOUR and DETAIL filters to the image "baboon.png". The code should show all the filtered images on a single figure.

15.9 Write a code to sharpen the image "baboon.png" with the factors of 0.8, 3.0, and 5.0. The code should show all the images on a single figure after sharpening.

15.10 Write a code to brighten the image "baboon.png" with the factors of 0.4, and 2.5. The code should show all the images on a single figure after brightening.

Chapter 16

GRAPHICAL USER INTERFACES

In this chapter, we will introduce the elements of a graphical user interface (GUI), and different options for inserting elements on a GUI. After covering the necessary information on GUIs, we will take a look at how to write callback functions for the elements of a GUI. And finally, we will present how to create different applications for different purposes.

Building a GUI is quite important in today's technological era. People may prefer to use GUIs for different applications compared to using just codes and scripts in interpreters; even though GUIs also work with codes and scripts. Python also possesses several toolkits to build GUIs such as tkinter, wxPython, PyQt, PyGTK. In this study, we will show how to create GUIs by making use of the tkinter toolkit.

"tkinter" is included in all versions of 3.1 and above for Windows, Linux, or Mac platforms. However, it has to be imported to the code in order to use the components or widgets within the toolkit.

16.1 Widgets

Widgets are the elements of the GUI. Most frequently used ones include *Button*, *Canvas*, *ChechButton*, *Entry*, *Frame*, *Label*, *LabelFrame*, *ListBox*, *Menu*, *MenuButton*, *Message*, *OptionMenu*, *PanedWindow*, *RadioButton*, *Scale*, *ScrollBar*, *SpinBox*, *Text*, and *Toplevel*.

We may create our first GUI and present a few widgets on it in the following.

Example 16.1 Write a code to create a GUI having a button, a *spinbox*, a *label* and a *canvas* on it.

Solution. The following code may be used to create the GUI.

```
#Example 16.1
#This example creates a GUI
from tkinter import * # *-->import everything from tkinter
root = Tk() #it creates the main window
root.title("This is TITLE")
# Creating widgets
Button1 = Button(root, bg='blue', text="Button1")# bg=background color
Spinbox1 = Spinbox(root, from_=0, to=5)
Label1 = Label(root,bg='red', text="This is just a LABEL")
Canvas1 = Canvas(root,bg='green')
#Putting created widgets on the main window by PACKING geometry manager
Canvas1.pack()#Canvas1 is located on the root
Button1.pack()#Button1 is located on the root
Label1.pack() #Label1 is located on the root
Spinbox1.pack()#Spinbox1 is located on the root
mainloop()#this holds everything appeared on the root
# until the object is closed
```

Listing 16.1: Example16p1.py

In all codes to be used for creating a GUI, "tkinter" has to be imported into the code. Also, **Tk()** should be assigned to a variable representing the main window, or the frame. After creating the main window, widgets can be produced and attached on the frame. To place the widgets on the frame, the **pack()** method may be used. With this method, the components are just packed on the frame. In addition, there exist the **grid()** and **place()**methods, which we will discuss in the next section. Once the entire code is written, *mainloop()* should be added to the code in order to hold everything to be displayed on the frame.

After running the code, we get the following output.

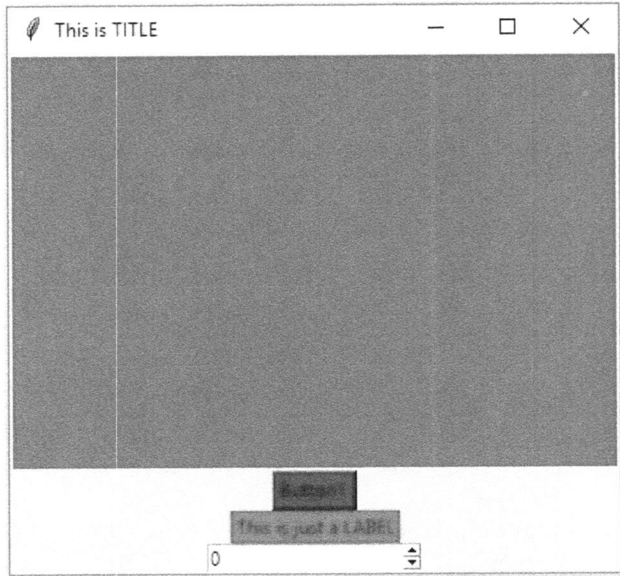

Figure 16.1: Output of Example 16.1

◀

As can be seen from the code, functions that are used for creating widgets have some features assigned to keywords. For example, the button function has a keyword "*bg*", which sets the background color of the Button widget. To see all the options about a widget, see the next example.

Example 16.2 Write a code that creates a *listbox* and assigns the following values to some of its features: Foreground color is blue, width is 20, height is 10, border width is 10, font is Courier, and font size is 20. The code should also list all available options of the *listbox* widget.

Solution. The following code may be used to accomplish the task.

```
#Example 16.2
#This example shows how to create a listbox and its options
from tkinter import *
root = Tk() #it creates the main window
listbox = Listbox(root,fg='blue',width=20, height= 10,
```

```
                    borderwidth=10, font=("Courier", 20))
listbox.pack()
listbox.insert(END, "First item")
MyList = ["Item two", "Item three", "Item four"]
#Add MyList to listbox
for item in MyList:
    listbox.insert(END, item)#add each item at the end
#show all features of the Listbox widget
for k in listbox.configure().keys():
    print(k, ':', listbox.cget(k))

mainloop()
```

Listing 16.2: Example16p2.py

Once the code runs, we will obtain the following result.

Figure 16.2: Output of Example 16.2

```
setgrid : 0
font : Courier 20
selectborderwidth : 0
```

```
width : 20
takefocus :
height : 10
listvariable :
borderwidth : 10
xscrollcommand :
bd : 10
highlightbackground : SystemButtonFace
relief : sunken
background : SystemWindow
exportselection : 1
fg : blue
state : normal
highlightcolor : SystemWindowFrame
yscrollcommand :
bg : SystemWindow
foreground : blue
selectmode : browse
cursor :
disabledforeground : SystemDisabledText
activestyle : underline
selectforeground : SystemHighlightText
highlightthickness : 1
selectbackground : SystemHighlight
```

◀

As it is seen from the list above, we may change many features of the *listbox* widget by just typing the keywords and the corresponding values inside the *Listbox* function.

Similarly, you can check and modify all the available options for different widgets only by changing the type of the widget in the code.

16.2 Geometry Manager

After creating the widgets, we need to display them on the main window. This can be achieved in one of the three ways including the pack method, place method, or grid method. In the first two examples, we have already seen how to show items on the screen by making use of the pack method.

The place method allows us to set the position and size of the units. However, it requires more attention to make the windows work within a pattern. For simple applications, the place method is not recommended.

The grid manager allows us to put the widgets on the GUI considering the positions of the rows and columns. It lines up the widgets like a table. It is the most popular method to be used for general purposes.

For the rest of the chapter, we will be using the grid method in our examples.

Assigning values for **row** and **column** numbers start from zero when the grid method is used. The keyword **sticky** sets the rotation of the widget, while the keywords **padx** and **pady** leave spaces horizontally and vertically in pixels.

Example 16.3 Write a code to enter the first name and last name in an entry. At the bottom, a submit button should be located. All widgets should be located using the grid method.

Solution. We can write the following code to accomplish the task.

```
#Example 16.3
#This example uses grid geometry method
from tkinter import *
root = Tk()
label1 = Label(root, text="First Name")
label1.grid(row=0, column=0, sticky=W, padx=1)
entry1 = Entry(root) #sticky --> N, NE, NW, W,E
entry1.grid(row=0, column=1, sticky=E,pady=5)
label2 = Label(root, text="Last Name")
label2.grid(row=1, column=0, sticky=W, padx=5)
entry2 = Entry(root)
entry2.grid(row=1, column=1, sticky=E,pady=5)
Button(root, text="Submit").grid(row=3, column=0, sticky=E)
```

```
root.mainloop()
```

Listing 16.3: Example16p3.py

Once the code runs, we will get the following output.

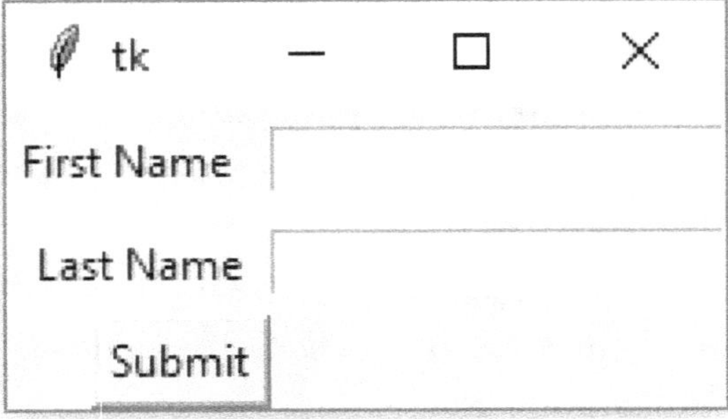

Figure 16.3: Output of Example 16.3

◀

16.3 Writing Callback Functions for Widgets

Callback functions are at the heart of GUI applications. Generally, they are triggered by a button. They are used for making connections among the widgets and concluding a result, or an event.

Example 16.4 Write a code that shows three meal options such as Pizza, Hot Dog, and Burger on a GUI. The interface should have some extras such as French Fries, Soda, etc. There needs to be a button to show the selected orders. Once the button is clicked, the selected options should be printed on the screen. The GUI should also have a button to terminate it once that button is clicked.

Solution. The following code can be used to construct the desired GUI.

```
#Example 16.4
#This example shows how to use Radiobutton and Checkbutton
from tkinter import *
root = Tk()
```

```
Btn1 = StringVar()
Var1 = IntVar()
Var2 = IntVar()
def MyCall():
    print("You selected ", Btn1.get())
    if Var1.get():
        print("Also you got French Fries")
    if Var2.get():
        print("Also you got Soda")
#Creating widgets
label1 = Label(root, bg="SkyBlue3", text="Select Your Meal :")
label2 = Label(root, bg="SkyBlue3", text="Extras :")
Rad1 = Radiobutton(root, text="Pizza", variable=Btn1, value="Pizza")
Rad2 = Radiobutton(root, text="Hot Dog", variable=Btn1, value="Hot Dog")
Rad3 = Radiobutton(root, text="Burger", variable=Btn1, value="Burger")
Chck1 = Checkbutton(root, text="French Fries", variable=Var1)
Chck2 = Checkbutton(root, text="Soda", variable=Var2)
B1 = Button(root, text='Show My Orders', command=MyCall)
B2 = Button(root, text='Quit GUI', command=root.quit)
#sticking widgets on GUI
label1.grid(row=0, column=0, sticky=W, padx=2, pady=2)
label2.grid(row=0, column=1, sticky=W, padx=30, pady=2)
Rad1.grid(row=1, column=0, sticky=W, padx=2, pady=2)
Rad2.grid(row=2, column=0, sticky=W, padx=2, pady=2)
Rad3.grid(row=3, column=0, sticky=W, padx=2, pady=2)
Chck1.grid(row=1, column=1, sticky=W, padx=30, pady=2)
Chck2.grid(row=2, column=1, sticky=W, padx=30, pady=2)
B1.grid(row=4, column=0, sticky=W, padx=2, pady=4)
B2.grid(row=4, column=1, sticky=E, padx=2, pady=4)
mainloop()
```

Listing 16.4: Example16p4.py

Above in the code, integer values can be assigned to the **value** keyword of the Radiobuttons, as well. If different integer values such as 1, 2, 3 are assigned, then, only one option can be picked over the GUI. If two values are the same and one is different, then, either one or two options can be picked together over the GUI.

Once the code runs, and the Hot Dog and Soda options are selected, we will get the following output.

Figure 16.4: Output of Example 16.4

And once the button is clicked, the following output will be displayed.

```
You selected  Hot Dog
Also you got Soda
```

◀

If Quit GUI button is clicked, then the interface is terminated.

Example 16.5 Write a code to create a GUI where the name of the user along with two numbers are entered into the interface. The interface should have a calculate button at the bottom left corner. Once the calculate button is clicked, the name and the result of the addition of the entered numbers should be displayed at the bottom right corner of the GUI.

Solution. We can write the following code to accomplish the task.

```
#Example 16.5
#This example shows getting entry values and display them on a label
from tkinter import *
def MyFunction():
    Result = Numbr1.get()+Numbr2.get()
    Showlabel['text']="Hello {} . The result is {}".\
```

```
    format(Name.get(), Result)
root = Tk()
root.title("My GUI")
Name = StringVar()
Numbr1 = DoubleVar()
Numbr2 = DoubleVar()
#set default values
Name.set("Your Name")
Numbr1.set("0")
Numbr2.set("0")
#Create widgets
Namelabel = Label(root, bg="SkyBlue3", text="Enter Your Name :",
               font=("Helvetica", 12,"bold"))
Sentclabel = Label(root, bg="SkyBlue3", text="Enter 2 Numbers to Add Below",
               font=("Helvetica", 12,"bold italic"))
Num1label = Label(root, bg="SkyBlue3", text="1st Number",
               font=("Helvetica", 12,"italic"))
Num2label = Label(root, bg="SkyBlue3", text="2nd Number",
               font=("Helvetica", 12,"italic"))
NameEntry = Entry(root, textvariable=Name, font=("Helvetica", 12))
Numbr1Entry = Entry(root, textvariable=Numbr1, font=("Helvetica", 12))
Numbr2Entry = Entry(root, textvariable=Numbr2, font=("Helvetica", 12))
CalcButn = Button(root, text="CALCULATE", command=MyFunction,
                  font=("Helvetica", 13,"bold"))
Showlabel = Label(root, bg="SkyBlue3", text="",
               font=("Helvetica", 12,"bold italic"))
#sticking widgets on GUI
Namelabel.grid(row=0, column=0, sticky=W, padx=2, pady=2)
NameEntry.grid(row=0, column=1, sticky=W, padx=10, pady=2)
Sentclabel.grid(row=1, column=0, sticky=E, padx=2, pady=2)
Num1label.grid(row=2, column=0, sticky=W, padx=2, pady=2)
Num2label.grid(row=2, column=1, sticky=W, padx=2, pady=2)
Numbr1Entry.grid(row=3, column=0, sticky=W, padx=2, pady=2)
Numbr2Entry.grid(row=3, column=1, sticky=W, padx=2, pady=2)
CalcButn.grid(row=4, column=0, sticky=W, padx=2, pady=2)
Showlabel.grid(row=4, column=1, sticky=W, padx=2, pady=2)
mainloop()
```

Listing 16.5: Example16p5.py

Once the code runs and the name and numbers are entered, we will obtain the following.

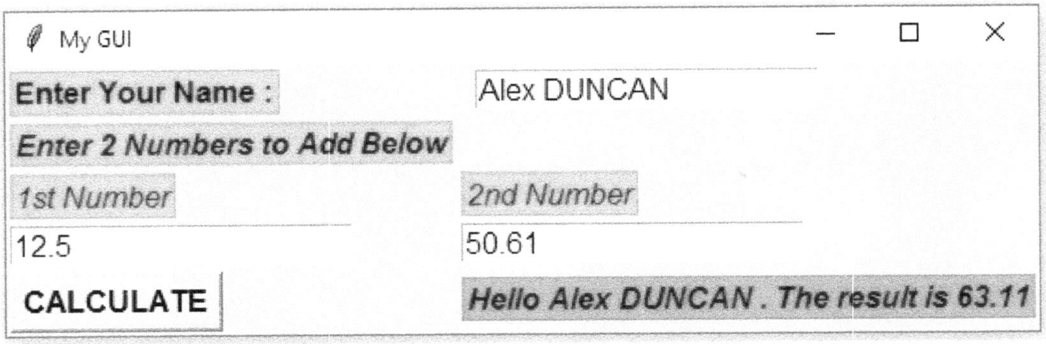

Figure 16.5: Layout of the GUI in Example 16.5

◀

Example 16.6 Write a code to create a GUI to be used for plotting the graphics of one of the functions including $\sin(x)$, $\cos(x)$, and $\tan(x)$ where $0 \leq x \leq 2\pi$. These three functions should be picked from a pop-up menu as y. Then, the graphics of $Z = A * y$ should be plotted where the value of A is linked to a slider. The slider should be assigned to 7 whose value can be selected between 0 and 10. y should be showing $\cos(x)$ once the graphics is plotted. The plot should be embedded within the GUI.

Solution. The following code may be used to accomplish the task.

```
#Example 16.6 —>this example shows how to plot a graph inside a GUI
from matplotlib.backends.backend_tkagg import FigureCanvasTkAgg as FigCan
from tkinter import *
import matplotlib.pyplot as plt
import numpy as np
def MyFunction(val):
    Namelabel3['text']="A = {}".format(val)
def Plotting():
    x = np.linspace(0,2*np.pi, 100) #creates 100 numbers
    A = Scale1.get()
    if dropVar.get()=="sin(x)":
        y = A * np.sin(x)
    elif dropVar.get()=="cos(x)":
```

```
        y = A * np.cos(x)
    else:
        y = A * np.tan(x)
    fig = plt.figure(figsize=(4,4))
    plt.plot(x,y,color="blue")
    plt.ylabel('y values',fontsize=12)
    plt.xlabel('x values',fontsize=12)
    plt.title('Graph of Z',fontsize=12);plt.grid(True)
    canvas = FigCan(fig, master=root)
    canvas.get_tk_widget().grid(row=1, column=2, sticky=SW, padx=2, pady=2)
    canvas.draw()
root = Tk()
dropVar=StringVar()
Namelabel1 = Label(root, bg="sky blue", text="Plotting the Graph of Z",
                  font=("Times", 12,"bold"))
Namelabel2 = Label(root, bg="sky blue", text="y =  ",
                  font=("Times", 13,"bold"))
Namelabel3 = Label(root, bg="sky blue", text="",
                  font=("Times", 14,"bold"))
Namelabel4 = Label(root, bg="sky blue", text="Z = A * y",
                  font=("Times", 14,"bold"))
Scale1 = Scale(root, from_=0.0, to=10, command=MyFunction,length=150,orient=VERTICAL)
optionList = ('sin(x)', 'cos(x)', 'tan(x)')
Options = OptionMenu(root, dropVar, *optionList)
Options.config(font=('Times',12),width=3, bg="sky blue")
PlotButn = Button(root, text="Plot Z", command=Plotting,
                    font=("Helvetica", 20,"bold"))
Canvas1 = Canvas(root, bg="white", width=400, height=400)
dropVar.set("sin(x)")#set the default value for OptionMenu
#sticking widgets on GUI
Namelabel1.grid(row=0, column=2, sticky=W, padx=50, pady=2)
Scale1.grid(row=1, column=0, sticky=W, padx=2, pady=2)
Options.grid(row=1, column=1, sticky=NE, padx=2, pady=2)
Namelabel2.grid(row=1, column=1, sticky=NW, padx=15, pady=10)
Namelabel3.grid(row=1, column=1, sticky=NW, padx=15, pady=50)
Namelabel4.grid(row=1, column=1, sticky=NW, padx=15, pady=90)
PlotButn.grid(row=1, column=1, sticky=SW, padx=5, pady=100)
Canvas1.grid(row=1, column=2, sticky=SW, padx=2, pady=2)
```

```
mainloop()
```

Listing 16.6: Example16p6.py

Once the code runs, $\cos(x)$ is selected from the pop-up menu. From the slider, 7 is selected and this value is assigned to A automatically. After clicking on the "Plot Z" button, we obtain the following layout.

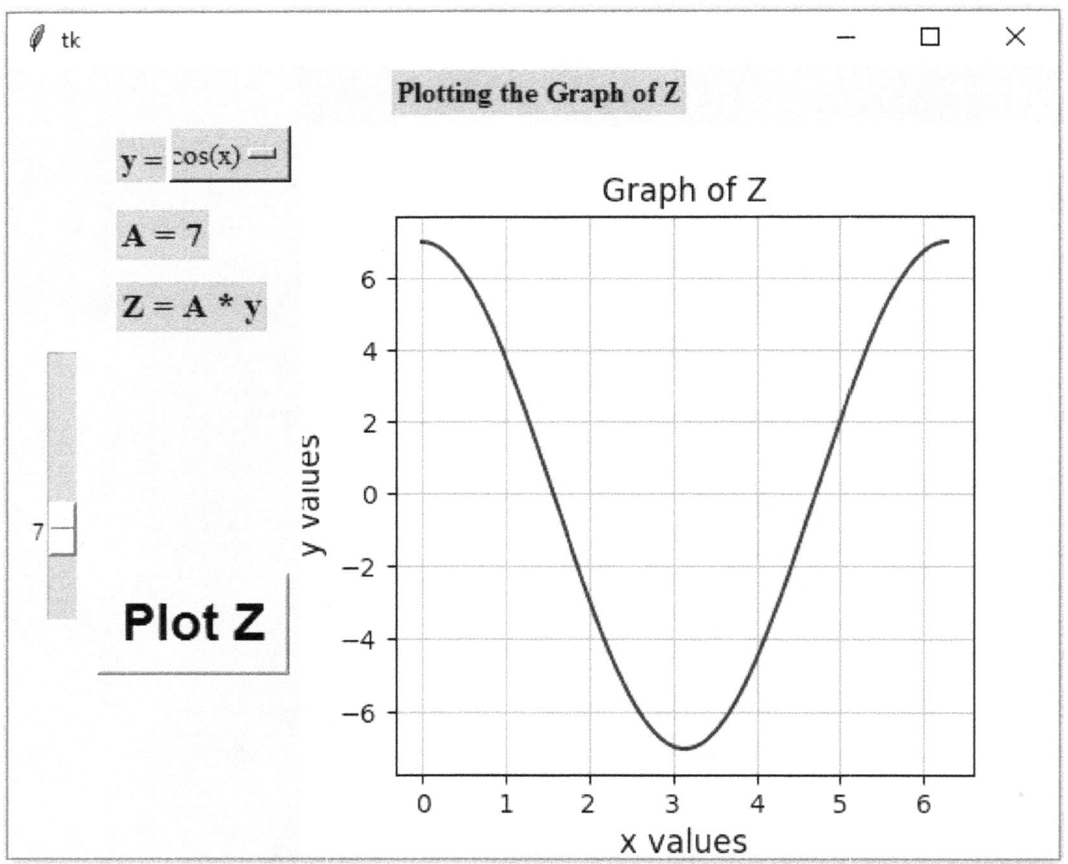

Figure 16.6: Layout of Example 16.6

16.4 Creating Menu

To create a menu on the GUI, the **Menu()** function is used. Then, by making use of "**add_command**", items can be added to the menu.

Example 16.7 Write a code to create a menu for a GUI. There should be "File" and "Help" menus on the GUI. "Open", "Save As", and "Exit" buttons should be inside the "File" menu, while the "Help" menu will involve "About" and "More Info" options.

Solution. The following code can be used to accomplish the given task.

```
#Example 16.7
#This example shows how to create menu in a GUI
from tkinter import *
from tkinter.filedialog import askopenfilename, asksaveasfilename
root = Tk()
def Helping():
    print("Helping")
def OpenFile():
    Folder = askopenfilename()
def SaveAsFile():
    Folder = asksaveasfilename()
Menubar = Menu(root)
# creating pulldown menu
Filemenu = Menu(Menubar, tearoff=0)
Filemenu.add_command(label="Open", command=OpenFile)
Filemenu.add_command(label="Save As", command=SaveAsFile)
Filemenu.add_separator()
Filemenu.add_command(label="Exit", command=root.quit)
Menubar.add_cascade(label="File", menu=Filemenu)
# creating another menu
Helpmenu = Menu(Menubar, tearoff=0)
Helpmenu.add_command(label="About", command=Helping)
Helpmenu.add_command(label="More Info", command=Helping)
Menubar.add_cascade(label="Help", menu=Helpmenu)
root.config(menu = Menubar)
# create a canvas
frame = Frame(root, width=200, height=200)
frame.grid(row=0, column=0, sticky=W, padx=2, pady=2)
```

```
mainloop()
```

Listing 16.7: Example16p7.py

Once the code runs and the File menu is clicked, we obtain the following layout.

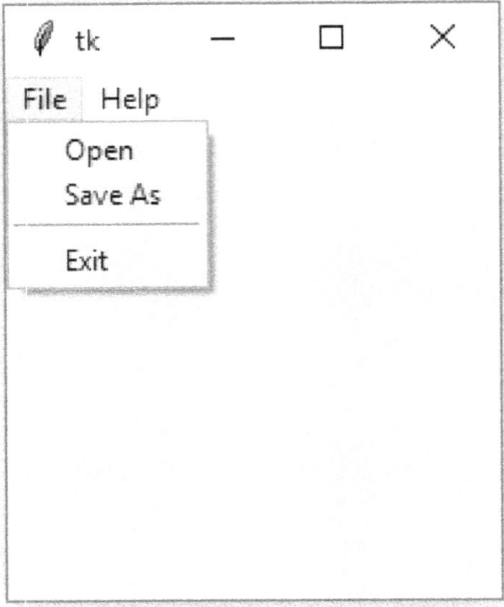

Figure 16.7: Layout of Example 16.7

16.5 Creating Applications

As seen from the examples considered so far, there are many widgets available for creating different applications in *tkinter*. Before creating a GUI, we need to know the purpose of the GUI so that we can design the layout of the interface and the content.

In this section, we will write codes to create GUIs for different applications in order to address the needs of various fields.

In Example 4.10, we produced a guess game. In this chapter, we will remake the example using an interface.

Example 16.8 Write a program that guides the user to guess the number picked by the computer between 1 and 100. The program should guide the user with commands such as "Go Down" or "Go up" by the labels sticked on a GUI. The GUI should show the number of trials on the interface as well.

Solution. The following code may be used to accomplish the task.

```
#Example 16.8
#This example has a guess game
from tkinter import *
import random
PickedNumber = random.randint(1,100)
Counter = 1
def StartGuess():
    global PickedNumber, Counter
    Gues = Numbrl.get()
    if (Gues == PickedNumber):
        Messaging = "CONGRATULATIONS!!! You got it in your {} th try".format
    (Counter)
        GuessButton.configure(state=DISABLED)
        PlyAgainButton.configure(state=NORMAL)
    elif (Gues > PickedNumber):
        Messaging = "Go DOWN..."
    else:
        Messaging = "Go UP..."
    MessageLabel['text'] = Messaging
    Counter += 1
def PlayAgain():
    global PickedNumber, Counter
    GuessButton.configure(state=NORMAL)
    PlyAgainButton.configure(state=DISABLED)
    Counter = 1
    PickedNumber = random.randint(1,100)
root = Tk(); root.title("Guess Game")
Numbrl = IntVar()
HeadLabel = Label(root, bg="DarkSlateGray1", text="GUESS GAME",
                  font=("Couries", 20))
SubLabel = Label(root, bg="DarkSlateGray1", text="Maximum Guessable Number
    is 100",
                  font=("Couries", 14))
```

```
GuessLabel = Label(root, bg="DarkSlateGray1", text="Please Enter Your Guess",
                   font=("Couries", 14))
GuesEntry = Entry(root, textvariable=Numbr1, width=3, font=("Helvetica", 15))
GuessButton = Button(root, text="GUESS", command=StartGuess,
                      font=("Helvetica", 16, "bold"))
PlyAgainButton = Button(root, text="Play Again", command=PlayAgain,
                      font=("Helvetica", 16, "bold"), state=DISABLED)
MessageLabel = Label(root, bg="DarkSlateGray1", fg="red", text="",
                   font=("Couries", 18))
HeadLabel.grid(row=0, column=1, sticky=E, padx=2, pady=2)
SubLabel.grid(row=1, column=1, sticky=E, padx=2, pady=2)
GuessLabel.grid(row=2, column=1, sticky=W, padx=2, pady=2)
GuesEntry.grid(row=2, column=1, sticky=W, padx=230, pady=2)
GuessButton.grid(row=3, column=1, sticky=W, padx=2, pady=2)
PlyAgainButton.grid(row=3, column=1, sticky=W, padx=150, pady=2)
MessageLabel.grid(row=4, column=1, sticky=W, padx=2, pady=2)
mainloop()
```

Listing 16.8: Example16p8.py

As seen above, global variables are used to define the variables and their correct values are being used inside and outside the functions as well. The code can be written without global variables using the class structure in an object-oriented manner as we did in Chapter 8. But, to keep it simple, the procedural oriented style is preferred for all users and programmers.

After running the code five times, we obtain the following output.

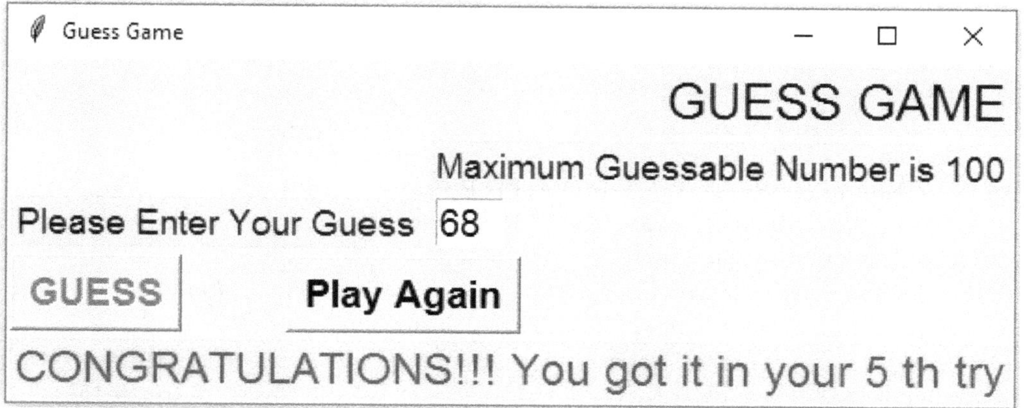

Figure 16.8: Output of Example 16.8

◀

As seen from the layout above, "GUESS" button is disabled and "PlayAgain" button is activated. Once "PlayAgain" is clicked, then "GUESS" button becomes active and "PlayAgain" button is deactivated again.

Example 16.9 Write a code to create a GUI for calculating the price of the orders for a restaurant. The interface should show the logo of the restaurant, 3 different meals such as "Hot Dog", "Burger", and "Pizza" having prices 9$, 8$ and 7$ respectively. On the interface, the tip should also be entered. **Spinbox** should be used to enter the number of orders for each meal. There should be a button displaying the amount of money for the payment on the interface.

Solution. We can write the following code to accomplish the task.

```
#Example 16.9
#This example creates a GUI for a restaurant
from tkinter import *
from PIL import Image, ImageTk
def CalcTotal():
    Tips = float(TipEntry.get())
    HotDogPr = int(HotDogSpinbox.get())
    BurgerPr = int(BurgerSpinbox.get())
    PizzaPr = int(PizzaSpinbox.get())
```

```
    TotalPrice = HotDogPr*9 + BurgerPr*8 + PizzaPr*7 + Tips
    Messaging = "Total Amount : {}".format(TotalPrice)
    TotalLabel['text'] = Messaging
root = Tk(); root.title("I WAS Restaurant")
Tips = DoubleVar();Tips.set("0")
HotDogPr = IntVar();BurgerPr = IntVar();PizzaPr = IntVar()
img = ImageTk.PhotoImage(Image.open("RestaurantLogo.png"))
Logo = Label(root, image = img)
MealLabel = Label(root, bg="OliveDrab1", text="ORDERS :",font=20)
PricesLabel = Label(root, bg="OliveDrab1",font=("Couries", 13),
                    text=" HotDog-9$ / Burger-8$ / Pizza-7$ ")
HotDogLabel = Label(root, bg="OliveDrab1", text="Hot Dog :",font=15)
BurgerLabel = Label(root, bg="OliveDrab1", text="Burger :",font=15)
PizzaLabel = Label(root, bg="OliveDrab1", text="Pizza :",font=15)
HotDogSpinbox = Spinbox(root, width=3, from_=0, to=5, font=15)
BurgerSpinbox = Spinbox(root, width=3, from_=0, to=5, font=15)
PizzaSpinbox = Spinbox(root, width=3, from_=0, to=5, font=15)
TipLabel = Label(root, bg="OliveDrab1", text="Tip :",font=15)
TipEntry = Entry(root, width=5, textvariable=Tips, font=12)
TotalLabel = Label(root, bg="DarkSlateGray1", fg="red", text="",font=22)
CalcButton = Button(root, text="Calculate TOTAL",
                    command=CalcTotal, font=("Couries", 15))
Logo.grid(row=0, column=0, sticky=W, padx=2, pady=2)
MealLabel.grid(row=1, column=0, sticky=W, padx=2, pady=2)
PricesLabel.grid(row=1, column=0, sticky=SE, padx=2, pady=2)
HotDogLabel.grid(row=3, column=0, sticky=W, padx=2, pady=2)
BurgerLabel.grid(row=3, column=0, sticky=W, padx=170, pady=2)
PizzaLabel.grid(row=3, column=0, sticky=E, padx=150, pady=2)
HotDogSpinbox.grid(row=3, column=0, sticky=W, padx=100, pady=2)
BurgerSpinbox.grid(row=3, column=0, sticky=W, padx=260, pady=2)
PizzaSpinbox.grid(row=3, column=0, sticky=E, padx=90, pady=2)
TipLabel.grid(row=5, column=0, sticky=W, padx=2, pady=2)
TipEntry.grid(row=5, column=0, sticky=W, padx=80, pady=2)
CalcButton.grid(row=6, column=0, sticky=W, padx=2, pady=2)
TotalLabel.grid(row=6, column=0, sticky=W, padx=180, pady=2)
root.mainloop()
```

Listing 16.9: Example16p9.py

Once the code runs, we obtain the following output.

Figure 16.9: Output of Example 16.9

16.6 PROBLEMS

16.1 Write a code to create a GUI having two buttons and 2 spinboxes using the grid geometry manager.

16.2 Write a code to create a listbox that has the following features: The foreground color is red, width is 15, height is 15, border width is 15, font is Times, and font size is 15.

16.3 Write a code to enter the first and last names in an entry. At the bottom, the submit button should be located. Once this button is clicked, the code should display the entered information on the GUI, as well.

16.4 Write a code that shows two meal options such as Fish and Beef on a GUI. The interface should also have extras such as French Fries, Desserts, and Soda. There must be a button showing the selected orders. Once this button is clicked, the selected options should be printed on the interface.

16.5 Write a code to create a GUI for plotting the graph of

$$y = 2 + \sin(A * x)$$

where $0 \leq x \leq 2\pi$ and the value of A is linked to a slider. The value of the slider should be selective between 0 and 10. There should be a button for plotting the graph of y. The graph should be embedded within the GUI.

16.6 Write a code to create a menu for a GUI. There should be "File", "Edit" and "Help" menus on the GUI. "Open", and "Save As" buttons should be inside the "File" menu; "Copy" and "Paste" buttons should be within the "Edit" menu; while the "Help" menu will have an "About" option alone.

16.7 Write a program to create a GUI for a simple calculator. The interface should have all numbers from 0 to 9, four main mathematical operations, an "=" button to show the result, and a "C" button to clear the screen of the calculator.

Bibliography

[1] https://docs.python.org/3/

[2] Cormen, Thomas H. and Stein, Clifford and Rivest, Ronald L. and Leiserson, Charles E., Introduction to Algorithms, 2001, 0070131511, 2nd, McGraw-Hill Higher Education

[3] http://www.python-course.eu/

[4] https://www.coursera.org/specializations/python

[5] https://docs.scipy.org/doc/numpy-dev/user/numpy-for-matlab-users.html

[6] https://www.programiz.com/python-programming/

[7] http://www.astroml.org/

[8] Ivezic, Zeljko and Connolly, Andrew J. and VanderPlas, Jacob T. and Gray, Alexander, Statistics, Data Mining, and Machine Learning in Astronomy: A Practical Python Guide for the Analysis of Survey Data, 2014, 0691151687, 9780691151687, Princeton University Press, Princeton, NJ, USA

[9] https://people.duke.edu/ ccc14/sta-663/

[10] Jonathan E. Guyer and Daniel Wheeler and James A. Warren, FiPy: Partial Differential Equations with Python, IEEE, 2009, Computing in Science & Engineering, 11, 3, 6-15, http://www.ctcms.nist.gov/fipy

[11] http://sam-dolan.staff.shef.ac.uk/mas212/notebooks/ODE_Example.html

[12] `http://www.pics4learning.com`

[13] `https://pillow.readthedocs.io/en/4.0.x/`

[14] `https://media.readthedocs.org/pdf/pillow/latest/pillow.pdf`

[15] Thomas, George B. and Weir, Maurice D. and Hass, Joel R. and Giordano, Frank R., Thomas' Calculus Early Transcendentals (11th Edition) (Thomas Series), 2005, 032119800X, Addison-Wesley Longman Publishing Co., Inc., Boston, MA, USA

[16] Moore, Holly, MATLAB for Engineers, 2014, 0133485978, 9780133485974, 4th, Prentice Hall Press, Upper Saddle River, NJ, USA

[17] McAndrew, Alasdair, A Computational Introduction to Digital Image Processing, Second Edition, 2015, 1482247321, 9781482247329, 2nd, Chapman & Hall/CRC

[18] Model, Mitchell L., Bioinformatics Programming Using Python: Practical Programming for Biological Data, 2009, 059615450X, 9780596154509, 1st, O'Reilly Media, Inc.

Index

www.ingramcontent.com/pod-product-compliance
Lightning Source LLC
Chambersburg PA
CBHW080404060326
40689CB00019B/4128

* 9 7 8 1 5 4 3 1 7 3 8 3 3 *